BRIGHT NOTES

THE PRINCE AND THE PAUPER BY MARK TWAIN

Intelligent Education

Nashville, Tennessee

BRIGHT NOTES: The Prince and the Pauper
www.BrightNotes.com

No part of this publication may be used or reproduced in any manner whatsoever without written permission, except in the case of brief quotations in critical articles and reviews. For permissions, contact Influence Publishers http://www.influencepublishers.com.

ISBN: 978-1-645423-36-2 (Paperback)
ISBN: 978-1-645423-37-9 (eBook)

Published in accordance with the U.S. Copyright Office Orphan Works and Mass Digitization report of the register of copyrights, June 2015.

Originally published by Monarch Press.
Charles L. Leavitt, 1966
2020 Edition published by Influence Publishers.

Interior design by Lapiz Digital Services. Cover Design by Thinkpen Designs.

Printed in the United States of America.

Library of Congress Cataloging-in-Publication Data forthcoming.
Names: Intelligent Education
Title: BRIGHT NOTES: The Prince and the Pauper
Subject: STU004000 STUDY AIDS / Book Notes

CONTENTS

1) A Biographical Sketch of Mark Twain	1
2) Introduction to Mark Twain	9
3) Textual Analysis	
Chapters 1–14	13
Chapters 15–33	28
4) Character Analyses	46
5) Critical Commentary	51
6) Essay Questions and Answers	58
7) Critical Battle Over Mark Twain's Psyche	65
8) Subject Bibliography and Guide to Research Papers	76

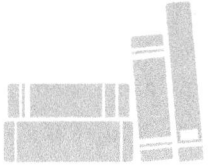

THE PRINCE AND THE PAUPER

A BIOGRAPHICAL SKETCH OF MARK TWAIN

INTRODUCTION

The story of Mark Twain's life is typical of the success stories written by Horatio Alger, the boys' novelist, for Twain had to struggle with an environment that seemed to be against him from the beginning. Born Samuel Langhorne Clemens in the one-horse village of Florida, Missouri, in 1835, he rose to become a world famous writer, lecturer and traveler before he died in 1910. Most of his success stemmed from a combination of indomitable drive, unceasing energy and maximum use of his own talents. He did have some good luck, too, and that helped.

EARLY LIFE

The facts of Twain's life are well known. Four years after he was born the family moved to Hannibal, Missouri, a village larger — but not a great deal different from — his birthplace. During his boyhood he had all the advantages and disadvantages of growing up in a country environment. He was close to the Mississippi

River, and probably spent a lot of time exploring its wooded shores and islands. He grew up in tune with the life around him, swimming and playing hooky from school, falling in love, and reading adventure stories. His family was an intelligent though not a wealthy or successful one by any material standards. Upon his father's death in 1847 Sam Clemens was apprenticed to his brother Orion, who owned a local printing shop and a newspaper. (Neither Orion, nor Twain's other brother, Henry, was able to break out of the poverty to which their impulsive and "wishful-thinking" schemes to make big money fast had doomed them.) Sam, however, left Hannibal to follow his trade over a good part of the country, working in towns as different as Keokuk and New York. But the pay wasn't too good for printers in those days, so he thought he'd go to South America and look for gold, or find some other way of making a quick fortune. Had he been successful in leaving the U. S., we would probably never have heard more of him.

LIFE ON THE MISSISSIPPI

Fortunately for American literature, however, Sam never took ship at New Orleans. He had become friendly with a river pilot named Horace Bixby, who promised to teach him about the Mississippi River. Bixby was a good pilot, one who loved his work and established a reputation for excellence. The story of Twain's apprenticeship is told in *Life on the Mississippi*, where he recounts his sudden awakening to the fact that pilots of river boats did more than just stand around looking "gaudy" after the boat had pulled into a landing. If, however, the romantic image of the pilot was gone from Twain's experience forever, it was replaced by an appreciation of the deep beauties of the river, its many shifts and changes, different at various times of the day, and sometimes unrecognizable from one season to the next. The account Twain leaves us is "stretched" somewhat, as Huck Finn would say, but in general the impression it creates is a true one.

LATER TRAVELS

After piloting the river steamers for about four years, Clemens retired to the Nevada gold country because the onset of the Civil War had put an end to river commerce. He prospected and clerked, doing many things to keep body and soul together. Eventually he ended up back in the printing trade, working his way from town to town before more or less settling down in California. He wrote short pieces for the newspapers he worked on, establishing a reputation as a humorist among the provincial readers of the Old West. So successful were these pieces, generally burlesques of social customs and institutions, that his newspaper sent him on a tour of the Sandwich Islands, as Hawaii was called in those days. He wrote a series of travel-letters burlesquing the typical travelogues tourists and professional travellers were sending back to their home towns from abroad. The result of this writing and some lecturing was that he began to be known as an earthy humorist, and classed among such writers as Bret Harte, Artemus Ward, and Petroleum V. Nasby. These men were known for their extremely popular western tales woven from folk stories and written in dialect with rough-hewn humor and plenty of recognizable concrete detail.

THE INNOCENTS ABROAD

In 1869 he published *The Innocents Abroad,* an account of a trip to Europe made under the sponsorship of a newspaper. In this book, he satirizes the folly of going across the Atlantic to see dead men's graves when there were many more living things to see in America, a dynamic and growing nation in contrast to decaying and dying Europe. The book made him famous, and gave him a literary reputation in the East. This reputation opened to him the doors of the cultivated and genteel literary patrons who generally scorned the writings of the Western humorists.

MARRIAGE

As a successful writer he attained respectability enough to marry into a wealthy Buffalo, New York, family. His wife was Olivia Langdon, of the socially prominent Langdons. Many aspects of their courtship, preserved for us in Twain's letters to Olivia and to her friends, remind us of the courtship of Tom and Becky in *Tom Sawyer*. Twain depended on "Livy" to read and censor his manuscripts before they were sent to the printer to make certain they contained nothing that would be improper among the social class he was now a member of. Some critics hold that this censorship did Twain a great deal of harm; others, who examined the surviving manuscripts, point out that "Livy" generally did not suggest more than minor changes, none of which significantly altered the books in question.

Five years after his marriage, Twain moved to Elmira, New York, and then to Hartford, Connecticut, where he had his famous and unusual house, an obvious status symbol, built. Most of his time was taken up with writing, although he did become involved in several get-rich-quick business enterprises that from then until the end of his life drained his energy and his finances, with the loss of not only most of his fortune but of "Livy's" as well.

FRIENDSHIP WITH DEAN HOWELLS

Twain had made friends with a number of interesting literary people, among them William Dean Howells, the famous author *(The Rise of Silas Lapham)* and editor *(The Atlantic Monthly).* Howells was quick to see and appreciate Twain's talent for humor, and encouraged him to develop the talent by acting as his literary adviser and practically guaranteeing Twain the critical backing of the prestigious *Atlantic.*

During this period he wrote *Roughing It* and *The Gilded Age.* The former is a memoir of the early days of the West; the latter, written in collaboration with Charles Dudley Warner, another friend, is a satire on the way the federal government was run in those days. By 1875 he was working sporadically on his first full length novel, *Tom Sawyer.*

HUCKLEBERRY FINN

The only other book that earned Twain more money than *Tom Sawyer* was its sequel, *Huckleberry Finn.* He began writing Huck Finn's story in 1876, and although this is the work on which the largest proportion of his literary fame rests, he found writing it to be hard going. The book was laid aside several times, but each time it was picked up again and brought a little nearer to completion. It did not appear until 1884 in England and 1885 in America. It was an immediate success, despite adverse criticism by some of the more conservative literary judges of the day who felt it was vulgar and dealt with insignificant material.

OTHER WRITINGS

Between 1876 and 1885 Twain had written several books, among them *The Prince and the Pauper, A Tramp Abroad,* and *Life on the Mississippi.* The first of these is a children's book which has as its basic plot a fictitious story of mistaken identity in which Edward VI of England is replaced on the throne by Tom Canty, a commoner. A thoroughly delightful book, *The Prince and the Pauper* was never one of Twain's more financially successful works. *A Tramp Abroad* is another travel book, this time recounting Twain's walking tour through Europe. And *Life on the Mississippi* is an account of Twain's visit to the scene of his early piloting days some twenty-five to thirty years after he left the trade. The work contains a great deal of pleasant reminiscence, social criticism, and much autobiographical material.

After *Huckleberry Finn,* Twain's next major work was *Pudd'nhead Wilson* (1889), a novel which has been published under the title *Natural Son,* which should give you some idea of its contents. Then came *A Connecticut Yankee in King Arthur's Court* (1894), a story about a Yankee engineer who goes back in time and becomes an adviser to King Arthur, enemy to Merlin, and — for all practical purposes — ruler of England until his reforms and charities are overthrown by the ignorant masses led by superstitious knights and clergy.

FINAL YEARS

Mark Twain's final years were not full of the satisfactions a man hopes to enjoy at the end of a life well led. Instead, he suffered a series of financial disasters and personal losses which would have taken the heart out of a lesser man. His publishing company failed in 1894 in spite of early successes — it had paid General Grant's widow $200,000, the largest payment in advance royalties ever paid, and it had reaped much from Twain's own works. Twain also invested a great deal of money in a typesetting machine invented and designed by a man named Paige who did not have to work too hard to convince exprinter Twain of the need for such an invention. Unfortunately, Paige stretched out the development of the machine, making costly changes and modifications that not only ran up 'the expenses, but delayed the finishing of the invention until Mergenthaler had produced his Linotype. Twain lost his proverbial shirt.

In spite of his advanced years — he was in his sixties — Twain undertook a foreign lecture tour to pay back every cent he owed. Since he was paid about $1,000 a night, it was not long before he was out of debt. But before he finished the tour, in 1898, there began for him a series of losses that were to color the rest of his life. These were deeper losses, more personally tragic than mere financial ruin. First, his daughter Suzy died, then his wife died, then his daughter Clara went with her husband to live in Europe. This left him with only his daughter Jean, whose epilepsy resulted in a fatal heart attack in 1910. Twain was now bereft of the company he enjoyed most, his girlish family. Four months after Jean's death, on April 21, 1910, Mark Twain suffered a heart attack and died. Disillusioned by business reversals and personal losses, he was a bitter writer toward the end of his days. The acidity of his earlier works was sweet when compared to his later bitterness, which became a violent cynicism and materialistic humanism. Some of his later writings, withheld from the public by his estate because of the savage nature of their biting satire, are just being published.

EVALUATION

His writings, from the earliest to those now appearing, can best be described as "iconoclastic." Twain delighted in shattering the images of glamor and romance built up around what he regarded as false and villainous institutions and customs, As a satirist attacking fraudulent pursuits and the weak, insipid facades of hypocrisy, Twain was a terrible enemy to injustice and confusion.

Many of his attacks seem unreasonable to us with sixty or seventy years of hindsight from which to judge. But Twain's attitudes were colored not only by his times and his lack of formal training, but also by his personality, which has been described by one critic as that of "neurotic genius."

INTRODUCTION TO MARK TWAIN

BRIEF SUMMARY

Two boys are born in London, about the middle of the sixteenth century. One-Edward, Prince of Wales-has been long awaited by the English nation. He is soon clothed in splendid robes. The other-Tom Canty-is unwanted by his poverty-stricken parents. He is poorly dressed, and he is soon covered with the dirt of his home in Offal Court. As soon as the boy is old enough, Tom's father, John Canty, forces his son to beg in the streets of London each day. When the fifteen-year-old boy returns home at night with little or no money, his father beats him. By a lucky accident, Tom learns to read, and he delights in learning about the wonderful world beyond the slums of London. Gradually, he begins to imagine that he is a prince. He so impresses many of the young people near his home that a small court is formed, and he acts in a royal manner toward his followers. At night, he dreams of the glories of being a prince; in the morning, he awakens to the filth and rough noises of Offal Court. Quite by accident, one day, he sees Prince Edward beyond the palace gates. When a soldier hits Tom, Prince Edward is angered and orders Tom to go with him into the royal palace. Edward is fascinated by Tom's stories of the freedom of his life, whereas Tom confesses that he has long wanted to be a prince. The two boys change clothing, only to find that in the mirror opposite them there seems to be no change whatsoever. Evidently, the two youths strongly resemble each other. Through a mischance, Prince Edward, still dressed as a pauper, is rudely thrust into the streets of London, where he amuses a howling and delighted mob with his announcement that he is the Prince of Wales. Tom Canty, in royal dress, is taken to see Henry VIII, who cannot understand why the youngster seems to have lost all memories of his past life. Princess Elizabeth and Lady Jane Grey try to be friendly with Tom. Earlier, the king had given the Great Seal of England to his son for a plaything. When Tom is asked to return the seal, he claims he has no knowledge of it. This helps convince Henry VIII that his son has lost his mind.

Edward is found by John Canty and is brought to Offal Court. Meanwhile, the king dies. Tom Canty, thought to be the heir to the throne, is saluted by both the nobles and the people as the King of England.

The circumstances of the two boys are in wide contrast. Tom is the central figure of a grand procession to Guildhall in the old City of London. Edward is given a sound beating by John Canty before being sent to bed on the floor. In the middle of the night, John Canty, his family, and Edward flee, for, during the previous evening, John had savagely beaten a priest, when he dragged Edward to Offal Court. By a lucky accident, Edward escapes John Canty, when the two are forcing their way through crowds of celebrating Londoners. Edward VI is being declared king. At this point, the real Edward announces to the mob that he is the king. He is greeted by jeers and taunts. Suddenly, a protector (Miles Hendon) appears from the crowd. Miles thinks Edward has lost his mind, but he plays along with the youth and treats him like a king to humor him. Miles tells the boy of his own troubles. He was sent away from his father's home, and his younger brother Hugh was given preference by the father. The young king

(Edward) declares he will award Miles any favor he may ask. Miles asks the privilege of sitting in Edward's presence. (The man is weary because he is always standing when he is in the youth's presence).

Gradually, Tom Canty finds that he is enjoying his life as a monarch. He delights in being regally clad, in being admired and cheered by crowds of people, in being served dinner by dozens of servants, and in being able to order about the most important nobles of England. Meanwhile, while Miles Hendon is away buying a second-hand suit of clothes for his little friend, Edward is tricked into a trap set by John Canty. The boy is forced to join a band of traveling vagabonds. When Edward declares that he is King of England, he is made the butt of much ridicule. Edward escapes, is fed by a poor farm woman, is then held captive by an insane hermit, and, once again, is recaptured by John Canty.

Miles reappears and rescues his small friend. Miles and Edward travel toward Hendon Hall, where the eager Miles expects his father will offer him a warm welcome. At the hall, Miles finds that his father is dead, that the sweetheart of his youth (Edith) has married his younger brother Hugh, and that he (Miles) is denounced as an imposter. Miles is imprisoned in the stocks, and he insists on receiving a beating intended for the young Edward. In gratitude, the boy declares Miles to be an earl. Of course, the suffering but grateful man thinks the boy has lost his wits.

Finally, the two companions arrive in London, on the day before the coronation of King Edward VI. Tom Canty, as the supposed king, rides through the streets of London on his way toward Westminster Abbey to be crowned. His mother recognizes him, but he rudely turns her aside. His conscience bothers him so much over this misdeed that, for the rest of the procession, he is thoughtful and sorrowful. In Westminster Abbey, just as the crown is about to be placed on Tom Canty's head, a voice-Edward's-rings out, declaring Tom to be an imposter. Tom publicly declares the ragged Edward to be the real monarch. Edward proves that he is the rightful monarch by telling where he once hid the Great Seal of England. All ends happily. Miles is, in truth, an earl; he marries Edith soon after the death of his brother Hugh. Tom Canty lives a long and respected life known as the "King's Ward." Young King Edward VI dies within a few years after ascending to the throne; but while he reigns, he always remembers the eventful days when he was mistaken for a pauper.

THE PRINCE AND THE PAUPER

TEXTUAL ANALYSIS

CHAPTERS 1–14

CHAPTER 1: THE BIRTH OF THE PRINCE

Over four hundred years ago in the "city of London," two baby boys are born. The one infant, born to a "poor family of the name of Canty," is called Tom. The other child, born to a "rich family of the name of Tudor," is called Edward, Prince of Wales. The Canty family does not want another child. The Tudor family-in fact, all England-has, for a long time, looked forward to the arrival of Edward: "longed for him, and hoped for him, and prayed God for him." Tom Canty is dressed in rags; Edward Tudor is wrapped in silks and satins.

CHAPTER 2: TOM'S EARLY LIFE

Tom Canty lives not far from London Bridge, on a little street called Offal Court. The whole family occupies one room on the third floor. Only Tom's father and mother have a regular bed. All the rest of the family, including Tom, his father's mother, and his two sisters, Bet and Nan, are allowed to sleep wherever they wish on the floor. Each night, Tom and the others cover themselves up with parts of a blanket and bundles of dirty straw. Tom's mother and his fifteen-year-old twin sisters are good-hearted, but Mr. Canty and his mother are fiendish. They often get drunk, fight, and swear. The children are secretly taught by Father Andrew, a good old priest who lives in the house. Tom's life is a hard life, but he does not realize it, for it is the only life he has ever known. He is accustomed to the fact that when he comes home empty-handed at night, after begging all day, his father will beat him, and then his grandmother will beat him all over again. In the night, his mother will creep to his side with a crust of bread she has saved for him. Often, Tom listens to Father Andrew's old tales and legends, especially those about kings and princes. When Tom cannot sleep at night he lets his imagination run free, as he pictures himself leading the "charmed life of petted prince in a regal palace." He dreams of seeing a real prince. Tom's reading and dreaming about princely life has such a strong effect upon him that he begins to act the prince. All the younger and older people around him begin to consider him a "most gifted and extraordinary creature," all except his own family. Tom organizes his own private "royal court" among his friends. At night he continues to dream that he is a prince. In the morning, when he awakens, his unpleasant surroundings are a great contrast to the gorgeous scenes he had pictured in his dreams.

CHAPTER 3: TOM'S MEETING WITH THE PRINCE

One morning, Tom gets up hungry and still remembering the shadowy splendors of his night's dreams, as he wanders about the streets. He passes beyond the walls of the city of London and

THE PRINCE AND THE PAUPER

walks in front of palaces of rich nobles. He stops near a "majestic palace" - Westminster. Tom is impressed by the men who guard the gate. He starts to move past them so that he might better see a boy of his own age, who is playing inside the gate. Tom notes that the other boy is dressed in "clothing ... all of lovely silks and satins, shining with jewels." Tom Canty is delighted, for he is looking at a real prince. He dashes to a position near the gate, and one of the guards pushes him away. The young prince inside orders the gates open, so that Tom Canty, "the little Prince of Poverty" may join Edward Tudor "the Prince of Limitless Plenty." Edward takes Tom to a beautiful room in the palace which he calls his cabinet. As Tom eats, the prince asks him questions. When Tom refers to his father as not being kind, Edward mentions his father, Henry VIII, as having a "heavy hand." Edward adds that his father "spareth" him, except "with his tongue." Edward mentions his sister, the Lady Elizabeth, and his cousin, Lady Jane Grey. Also, he mentions his older sister, the Lady Mary. Tom tells Edward of the varieties of activities that go on in Offal Court, such as Punch-and-Judy shows, racing, swimming and dancing about the Maypole.

Edward is very much impressed by Tom's freedom. The Prince of Wales wishes that he might dress like Tom and "revel in the mud once." At Edward's command, the two lads change clothes with each other. They stand side by side before a great mirror. To their surprise, there does not seem to have been any change made. The prince remarks that the two boys have the "same hair ... same eyes ... same voice and manner ... same form and stature ... same face and countenance." Edward notices the bruise on Tom's hand. Anxious to punish the man-at-arms who rudely pushed Tom, the prince dashes out of the room, through the palace, and across the grounds-wearing Tom's dirty rags. The young boy orders the gates to be unbarred. No sooner is the poorly dressed Edward outside the gates than the soldier hits him on the ear. The crowd gathered about, laughs. The prince is indignant and claims that the soldier is to hang for hitting him. The man-at-arms says, mockingly: "I salute your gracious Highness." Then, calling the indignant Edward "crazy rubbish," the soldier orders the bewildered boy to leave. The crowd closes around Edward hustling him down the road, all the time hooting and shouting at him.

Comment (Chapters 1-3)

The first chapter emphasizes the keynote literary technique of the entire tale-contrast. Every desirable material thing that the Prince of Wales has, Tom Canty has not. Note Twain's rough jest, implied in the name of Tom Canty's street, Offal Court. Twain's wry humor is illustrated when he writes that many of the Canty family "were not restricted" as to sleeping quarters; they have "all the floor to themselves, and might sleep" where they choose. Twain often pairs up his characters. The prince and the pauper are a pair of a sort. Tom's sisters Bet and Nan are twins. In Chapter 2, Tom Canty's organized royal court somewhat resembles Tom Sawyer's gang in *Huck Finn*. Note the contrast between Tom's dreams and what he sees in the morning when he awakens. Charing Village is the site of the prominent Charing Cross (railroad) Station in London, today. In Chapter 3, note the use of the "outside-inside" technique for contrast: Tom in his rags is outside the palace fence; the prince in silks and satins is inside the barrier. One is reminded of the thought "Clothes make the man," when Edward says: "Now that I am clothed as thou wert clothed, it seemeth I should be able the more nearly to feel as thou didst." This is a **foreshadowing** of what young Edward actually will feel when he lives Tom's life.

CHAPTER 4: THE PRINCE'S TROUBLES BEGIN

After hours of persecution, the Prince of Wales is finally left to himself. When he became too tired to speak, his tormentors stopped bothering him. He stops near the Grey Friar's church, now a home for poor and forsaken children, newly named Christ Church. Edward asks some of the young boys to tell their master that he - Edward Prince of Wales - wishes to speak with him. The children make fun of Edward and direct their dogs to run at the little prince. Toward night, Edward is tired, bruised, bleeding, and his clothes are all covered with mud. He tries to find Offal Court, Tom's street. Suddenly, he is seized by a "great drunken ruffian" - Tom's father, John Canty. Edward declares again that he is the Prince of Wales. The surprised Canty drags the struggling prince homeward.

CHAPTER 5: TOM AS A PATRICIAN

As the Prince of Wales leaves his cabinet Tom begins to admire his reflection in a great mirror. After half an hour, he wonders why the prince has not returned. He thinks that perhaps someone will find him in the prince's clothes. The prince is not there to protect him and to explain why he is in the clothing. Tom opens the door; immediately six men and two young pages bow before him. Startled, he quickly shuts the door and paces the floor. Lady Jane Grey is announced. She asks him if something is the matter with him. He kneels to her and says that he is "only poor Tom Canty." Embarrassed, she asks the boy she believes to be the Prince of Wales not to kneel to her. She leaves. Soon the palace is filled with whispers: "The prince hath gone mad." An official proclamation is made that no one is to discuss "this false and foolish matter", that is, that the prince seems to have lost his mind. Tom finally finds himself in a beautiful chamber in which sits a "very large and very fat man" - Henry VIII - supposedly his father. The king treats him tenderly, taking the boy's face between his hands and gazing earnestly and lovingly into it awhile. Tom says to the king: "I am the meanest among thy subjects ... 'tis by a sore mischance and accident I am here." Tom thinks that everyone knows he is not the prince and that he will be killed for wearing the prince's clothing. When the king says: "Thou shall not die," Tom jumps up with joy and cries out: "I am not to die: the king hath said it!" The king questions Tom in Latin and in French. When the boy cannot respond in French, the king is distressed. The ruler explains that "Overstudy hath done this .... Away with his books and teachers .... Pleasure him with sports." At this time Henry VIII tells one of the nobles that he wishes Parliament to sentence Lord Norfolk to death. Tom, heavy-hearted, leaves the presence of the king. He now feels a captive, in a gilded cage.

CHAPTER 6: TOM RECEIVES INSTRUCTIONS

Back in the prince's rooms, Tom sits down. Eventually he is joined by Lord St. John, who delivers a message from the king. He is not to deny "that he is the true prince ... heir to England's greatness." He also is to stop speaking of "lowly birth and life." He is to be advised by Lord Hertford and Lord St. John "upon occasions of state." Tom agrees. Mention is made of the fact that there will be a banquet that very night which the prince is supposed to attend. Lady Elizabeth and Lady Jane Grey arrive and talk with Tom. He is pleased to learn that the two "little ladies" are to go with him to the Lord Mayor's banquet in the evening. Tom asks to take a nap. Every attempt he makes to help himself is hindered by one of many servants who insist on doing everything for him. Lord Hertford and Lord St. John discuss the lad while he rests. Lord St. John is surprised that he does not remember some of his languages. Lord Hertford tells his companion that it is treason to discuss this matter. After Lord St. John leaves, Lord Hertford falls into deep thought. He decides that the young lad sleeping on the bed cannot be an impostor, for no impostor would deny that he were the prince. The puzzled Lord concludes by saying: "This is the true prince, gone mad!"

CHAPTER 7: TOM'S FIRST ROYAL DINNER

Early in the afternoon Tom is dressed for dinner. All of his clothes are changed, from his ruff to his stockings. He sits in the middle of a large room where a table has been set for one. The boy does not realize that the numerous servants he sees in the room are only a part of his helpers, for he has three hundred and eighty-four servants besides these. All of the ones present in the room have been well drilled to remember "that Prince Edward is temporarily out of his head." Tom eats with his fingers. He has his napkin taken away, for fear it become soiled. He examines the turnips and lettuce, asking what they are. At the end of the meal he fills his pockets with nuts - the only thing which the servants allow him to do with his own hands during the meal. When his nose itches, he is very distressed, for he does not know what the rules of etiquette have to say about such an emergency. Finally, he scratches his nose himself. Everything else during the meal has been done for Tom. At the conclusion of the meal a finger bowl is brought to Tom. He drinks some of the fragrant rose-water in it. Just as the chaplain takes his place behind Tom's chair and lifts his hands and eyes heavenward, to begin a blessing, Tom, not noticing him, gets up and leaves the table. Back in his own room (that is, the Prince of Wales' own room) Tom tries on a suit of armor. When he finds some books in a closet about the etiquette of the English court, he settles down to learn more about his new life.

CHAPTER 8: THE QUESTION OF THE SEAL

About five o'clock in the afternoon Henry VIII realizes that he is about to die. One of his last wishes is that the Duke of Norfolk die. The Lord Chancellor asks for the Great Seal. Henry is reminded that he had given the Great Seal "into the hands of ... the Prince of Wales." A messenger tells the king that the prince "cannot recalled to mind that he received the Seal." The Chancellor takes with him Henry's small Seal. Parliament declares that the Duke of Norfolk will be beheaded the next day.

CHAPTER 9: THE RIVER PAGEANT

About nine o'clock in the evening the river, covered with boats and barges, is ablaze with light. The stone steps leading from the palace to the River Thames are filled with servants and soldiers. Nearly fifty barges, elaborately decorated, draw near the stone steps. From the palace gateway comes a procession of soldiers. A carpet is unfolded from the palace to the water. Trumpets sound. In order come the city guard, Knights of the Bath, judges, the Lord High Chancellor of England, and representatives of the French and Spanish courts. Lord Hertford appears and then, with his back to the river, steps backward as he bows at each step. He is bowing to "the high and mighty, the Lord Edward, Prince of Wales." Tom Canty hears the trumpet-blast and the proclamation which announces him to the people. On the top of the palace, bonfires are lit. Young Tom Canty, bred in the gutter of London, familiar with rags and dirt and misery, is now magnificently dressed and covered with precious jewels.

Comment (Chapters 4-9)

When Tom thinks of the reaction of the Offal Court herd to his marvelous tale, he realizes that they would say his overtaxed imagination has "at last upset his reason." (This is similar to people's reactions to Cervantes' main character, Don Quixote.) The picture of Henry VIII is the traditionally accepted one. Compare Tom's feeling that he is a captive (end of Chapter 5) with Edward's later reaction (in Chapter 10) that he is a prisoner. In Chapter 6, note Twain's Mississippi River talk in the description of Tom's conversation at court: "Snags and bars" grow "less and less frequent." Also, Tom's two "guardian angels" (Lord Hertford and St. John) feel "much as if they were piloting a great ship through a dangerous channel" as they guide Tom's conversations. Compare the thoughts of Lord Hertford concerning the identity of Tom (end of Chapter 6) with the musings of Tom's mother about Edward (in Chapter 10). "Benvenuto" refers to Benvenuto Cellini (1500-1571), the Italian artisan who created priceless art works in precious metals. Note the Mississippi River humor when Tom gets up and leaves the table, just as the chaplain elaborately prepares to pray. "Madam Parr, the queen," is the sixth (and last) of Henry VIII's six wives. (She outlived Henry and married again.) Tom's finding and reading the books about the etiquette of the English court is comparable to Huck Finn's reading some books he finds about European monarchies. Note that much of the description in Chapter 9 is quoted from an unindicated source.

CHAPTER 10: THE PRINCE IN THE TOILS

When Tom Canty's father drags Prince Edward into Offal Court, no one offers a word for the boy, except one man. This man tries to keep John Canty from beating the prince. The enraged

Canty hits the meddler over the head, and, with a groan, the unhappy man sinks to the ground. In the Canty's room, John Canty displays the boy to the entire family, as he says to him: "Name thy name. Who art thou?" The boys says: "I am Edward, Prince of Wales, and none other." Tom's mother and sisters are distressed that the lad seems to have lost him mind. The mother says: "Thy foolish reading hath wrought its woeful work at last and ta'en thy wit away." Prince Edward rejects her, saying: "Truly have I never looked upon thy face before." John Canty demands to know what the boy has gathered during the begging of the day. The boy replies: "Offend me not with thy sordid matters." At this answer the man strikes him. John Canty's mother helps her son beat the boy, as well as the girls and their mother. All go to bed. The young girls cover the prince "tenderly from the cold with straw and rags." Tom Canty's mother cannot sleep, for there is an undefinable something about this boy, that is lacking in Tom Canty. Her sharp mother-instinct makes her aware of this. She wants to make a test, in an attempt to prove whether this boy is her son or not, and thinks of a method. When Tom was a small child, some gunpowder burst in his face. Since that time, whenever he is "startled of a sudden out of his dreams or out of his thinkings ... he hath cast his hand before his eyes ... not as others would do it, with the palm inward, but always with the palm turned outward." Three different times Mrs. Canty awakens the boy, and three different times he makes no special movement with his hands. Even though she can accept the fact that Tom may be insane, she believes that "his hands are not mad," for they cannot "unlearn so old a habit in so brief a time."

During the night Prince Edward half awakens. He thinks that he is sleeping in his own princely chamber, surrounded by guards. He believes that he had dreamed of being changed to a pauper. He realizes that what he thought was a dream is a reality - that he is a prisoner in a den fit only for beasts. A knock at the door announces a messenger who claims that the man John Canty hit on his way home, the priest Father Andrew, is dying. The Canty family leave the household within five minutes. Each person is reminded that, if the group becomes separated, all will meet on London Bridge. The hurrying Cantys and the prince suddenly move from the darkness of night into the lights along the river front. John Canty keeps a strong hold on the prince. A burly waterman is shoved by Canty making his way through the crowd. The drunk riverman insists that Canty drink a toast to the Prince of Wales. While this is happening Prince Edward dives among the forest of legs about him and disappears. Realizing that a false Prince of Wales is attending the Lord Mayor's banquet, Edward heads toward the Guildhall, where he plans to denounce the impostor. He decides that young Tom Canty shall be hanged, drawn, and quartered.

CHAPTER 11: AT GUILDHALL

Tom Canty, the pauper, believed by the cheering crowds to be Edward, Prince of Wales, rides in the royal barge down the Thames. Everywhere there is music, bonfires, lights, and the flash and boom of artillery. After landing, Tom, in the midst of the procession, marches toward Guildhall. There he is received with due ceremony by the Lord Mayor and the Fathers of the City in the great hall. Many tables are filled with eager spectators. Tom drinks from a loving-cup, and the banquet begins. During the festivities, there are gorgeously dressed dancers. While the pauper (Tom) occupies the Prince of Wales' position, the real Prince Edward is outside the gates of Guildhall. The crowd is much amused by the lad who claims he is the prince. Suddenly, at Prince Edward's side stands a tall, trim-built, muscular man of about thirty years of age. He names himself Miles Hendon, and announces that he will protect Prince Edward. The crowd starts to oppose the stranger in the faded and threadbare clothing. Suddenly horsemen come charging down upon the mob, and a voice shouts: "Way for the king's messenger!" Inside the Guildhall, the announcement is made: "The king is dead!" For a moment, there is silence; then all sink to their knees and, stretching out their hands toward Tom, shout: "Long live the king!" An idea occurs to Tom. He loudly proclaims that "the king's law be law of mercy." Then he adds: "To the Tower and say the king decrees the Duke of Norfolk shall not die!"

CHAPTER 12: THE PRINCE AND HIS DELIVERER

Meanwhile, Prince Edward and his deliverer, Miles Hendon, head back toward London Bridge. Edward is grieved at the death of his father yet remembers that he is now king. London Bridge is a small town, complete unto itself. It connects two neighbors- London and Southwark. It has a single street a fifth of a mile long. People are born and die, sometimes, without ever having left the Bridge. These individuals naturally imagine that their world is the one great thing in the universe. On the iron spikes of the Bridge gateways are the decaying heads of beheaded "renowned men." Miles takes Edward to the little inn on the Bridge where he is staying. As they approach the building Tom Canty's father attempts to seize Edward by force. Miles forces Canty to withdraw. In Miles' chamber, Edward lies down on the bed and instructs Miles to call him when the meal is ready. Then the young king (at the death of his father he automatically became king) falls into a deep sleep. Miles looks carefully at the boy and decides that he will protect him - that he will be "his elder brother, and care for him and watch over him." Miles removes his cloak and wraps Edward in it. A meal is brought to the chamber. Edward awakens and thanks Miles for the use of his cloak. Standing in front of the washstand, Edward is somewhat irritated that Miles does not immediately help him wash before the meal. Miles, playing along with what he believes to be the boy's fantasy, does as Edward bids. To Miles' surprise, the lad does not want his deliverer (Miles) to sit at the table with him. To humor the lad, Miles stands behind him and waits upon him. All the time, Miles reminds himself that he "must humor the poor lad's madness." Edward questions his companion as to his background. Miles speaks of his wealthy father, "Sir Richard Hendon, of Hendon Hall, by Monk's Holm in Kent." He mentions his dead mother and his two brothers. They are Arthur, and older brother, with a beautiful soul; and Hugh, the younger brother, described by Miles as "a mean spirit," covetous, treacherous, vicious, underhanded-a reptile. Also, Miles describes Lady Edith, his cousin. When he was home, he loved her and she loved him but she was contracted in marriage to the older brother Arthur. Hugh, the younger brother, was in love - but with Lady Edith's fortune Miles describes himself as having led a wild life - "though 'twas a wildness of an innocent sort," which had in it no "taint of crime of baseness." Hugh, the younger brother, magnified Miles' faults. He placed a ladder in Miles' chambers, which convinced the father that Miles was about to carry off Edith and marry her, against the father's wishes. Miles' father banished him for three years. At the end of this time, Miles was taken captive. He spent seven years in a foreign dungeon. Free at last, Miles Hendon is heading back toward his home, Hendon Hall. At this point Edward tells his story. Miles thinks to himself that the child has a great imagination. Edward directs Miles to name his reward for having saved him (the king) from "injury and shame." Miles decides that he would like to be able to sit in the presence of the majesty of England. Tapping Miles on the shoulder with the sword, the little king says: "Rise, Sir Miles Hendon, knight." Then the young monarch adds: "Rise and seat thyself, thy petition is granted." Believing that the child is living in a world of the imagination, Miles says to himself: "I am become a knight of the Kingdom of Dreams and Shadows!"

CHAPTER 13: THE DISAPPEARANCE OF THE PRINCE

After eating, Edward directs his companion to remove his clothing for him. Miles is expected to sleep across the door and guard it. He does so. Upon awakening, Miles Hendon measures Edward for a different suit of clothing, using a string for a tape measure. Then Miles slips softly out of the room and returns about one-half hour later with a complete second-hand suit of boy's clothing. After some difficulty in threading the needle, the returned warrior mends the clothing for the boy. Deciding to awaken Edward, he approaches the bed, throws back the covers, and to his astonishment discovers that the boy is gone. He closely questions the servant at the inn, who tells him a youth had entered the building, after Miles' departure, and delivered a message that Miles wished the boy to join him immediately at the end of London Bridge, on the Southwark side. A "ruffian-looking" man was noted to be nearby. In a fury, Miles starts to hunt for Edward. He is pleased that Edward had answered a summons that he thought had come from Miles.

CHAPTER 14: LE ROI EST MORT-VIVE LE ROI

Tom Canty wakes up early in the morning. For a moment he thinks that all the festivities of the previous night have been a madcap dream. He begins to shout out to his two sisters, Nan and Bet. His shouts are answered by a gentlemen-in-waiting. Tom asks: "Who am I?" He is told that he is "Edward, king of England." Again, Tom sleeps and dreams. He imagines that he has found twelve bright new pennies, with which he surprises his mother at home. He awakens and finds that he is still a captive and a king. Then begins the long process of dressing. Each garment is handed from person to person before it reaches Tom. He becomes weary of the ceremony. When his stockings are about to be placed on him, the First Lord of the Bedchamber hurries the things back down the long line of attendants; it seems that there is a damaged string on the hose. After being dressed, Tom is taken to the Hairdresser-royal. After breakfast he goes to the throne room, where he is given reports on the kingdom. He is amazed that a great deal of money has been spent in running Henry VIII's household. Back in his private chambers, Tom enjoys talking with the two young ladies, Lady Elizabeth and Lady Jane Grey. His "elder sister" (Mary Tudor) talks with him for a brief time. Finally, a boy of twelve years of age (Humphrey Marlow) appears and reminds the "king" that he is his whipping boy. It seems that, in the past, whenever the Prince of Wales made a mistake in his studies, the whipping boy took his whipping for him. ("None may visit the sacred person of the Prince of Wales with blows.") Tom thinks to himself that he wishes a boy might be hired to take his "dressings for him" and he would take his own "lashings." The whipping boy reminds the sovereign that this is the day when he is to be whipped. Tom assures him that there will be no whipping. Humphrey Marlow is upset at the thought that the former Prince of Wales, now the king, will no longer need a whipping boy. Tom immediately appoints him "Hereditary Grand Whipping Boy to the royal house of England." Humphrey is encouraged by Tom to talk about life in the court. From this conversation Tom fills in background on what is happening. The lords of the council have decided that King Edward should dine in public, so that any gossip about his having lost his mind might be stilled. Lord Hertford asks Tom the location of the Great Seal. Tom does not know.

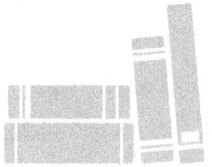

THE PRINCE AND THE PAUPER

TEXTUAL ANALYSIS

CHAPTERS 15–33

CHAPTER 15: TOM AS KING

During the next day Tom receives foreign ambassadors. He is very tired at the conclusion of the long and dreary speeches delivered for his benefit. By the end of the third day of his "kingship," he has begun to feel a little less uncomfortable about his new station. On the fourth day, he is to begin to dine in public. This business of dining with many eyes watching him worries Tom a but. From a window of the palace, Tom notes some agitation among members of the crowd along a nearby road. The "king" directs that a messenger find out what it is all about. Eventually, a man, a woman, and a young girl appear in front of Tom-for he is to judge the three. Tom recognizes the man as "the stranger that plucked Giles Witt out of the Thames." The man is accused of taking a man's life by poison. The evidence is very circumstantial. The man is terrified, because he is to be boiled alive, in punishment for being a poisoner. Tom is distressed at this punishment and suggests that the law be changed. The condemned man mentions the fact that, at the very time when he was supposed to be poisoning someone, he was saving the life of a drowning boy. Tom himself had witnessed this rescue. Tom Canty says: "Let the prisoner go free-it is the king's will." The surrounding members of the court are favorably impressed with Tom's intelligence and spirit. The woman and the little girl are ordered into the room. They are accused of having sold themselves to the devil and bringing about a "storm that wasted all the region around about." They are supposed to have caused the storm by pulling off their stockings. Tom sets the woman and her child free. Then he urged her to remove her stockings, in order to provoke a storm. The woman does so, but there is no storm.

CHAPTER 16: THE STATE DINNER

Gradually, Tom is getting accustomed to his new duties as king. The great banquet-room in which he is to dine is filled with brilliantly dressed people. The table is ceremoniously decorated, and Tom, accompanied by fifty courtiers, marches into the beautifully decorated chamber. He sits down, music is played, and food is served, course after course. Tom does not hurry, for he finds that he is enjoying the bright pageant.

Comment (Chapters 10-16)

John Canty's descriptive word for Edward's strange actions is "mummeries" - a ridiculous performance of playacting. In Chapter 10, John Canty with unkind humor demands that the family get on its knees to do Tom "reverence." This is somewhat comparable to Huck Finn's make-believe "reverence" for the duke and the king when he first meets them (in *Huck Finn*).

Compare Tom's mother's description of the reaction of her son when he is startled (in Chapter 10) to the actual occurrence of this reaction, when Tom later recognizes his mother (in Chapter 31). Notice the use of chiaroscuro-contrast in light and dark-when the Canty family steps from "darkness into light" near the Thames River. See Twain's "note" on the "loving-cup." In Chapter 11, compare and contrast the reactions of Tom and Edward to crowds of people: Tom admiring the "whirling turmoil of gawdy figures" and Edward being repulsed by the surging mob, which is amused at his attempts to enter Guildhall. Miles Hendon is called a champion, a defender of the rights of honor of someone else. Miles is described as a "stranger" (a Gothic character who is mysterious and unknown). Chapter 12 has a splendid little essay describing London Bridge, with a satirical Twain commentary on provincialism-excessive pride in one's own small environment. Miles thinks that Edward's mind "has been disordered with ill usage." Compare this with the courtiers' reactions to Tom's "strange" behavior. Miles speaks in soliloquy, that is, aloud to himself, in Chapter 12. He says he "must humor the poor lad's madness" (comparable to Huck Finn's humoring of his father, "Pap," as well as the king and the duke, in Huck Finn). Miles thinks of the "contrast" between his "glory" (he is now a knight) and his "raiment" (he is poorly dressed). Miles Hendon's **dramatic monologue** in Chapter 13 is typical of Twain's interest that literary technique, in which a character speaks to an audience which does not vocally respond (in this case, the reader). Whereas once Tom longingly dreamed of being a prince, now-sleeping in the royal bed-he dreams of being a carefree pauper. Edward's sister ("Bloody Mary") later succeeds him on the English throne where she, a devout Catholic, rules as Mary I from 1553-1558. Chapter 15 deals with Twain's satirical picture of the danger of justice based on imaginary and circumstantial evidence. The description of Tom eating dinner in state is supposedly quoted from the text of an "ancient chronicler." One cannot be sure whether Twain uses this descriptive method as an imaginative literary device, or whether he actually does cite an historical source.

CHAPTER 17: FOO-FOO THE FIRST

While Tom is enjoying the pageantry of his dinner, Miles Hendon hurries across London Bridge looking for a lost companion - the real King Edward. Miles attempts to figure out logically just what the boy would do. Probably he would escape from his father and go towards Miles' home, Hendon Hall. Meanwhile, the young King Edward has been directed to a forest. The king and his companion enter a ruined barn in the middle of the woods. They are soon joined by John Canty in disguise. John tells the king that he has decided to change his last name to Hobbs. He tells the young boy to change his name to Jack. Edward goes to sleep in the corner under a pile of old dirty straw. When he awakens, he sees a strange group of "ruffians, of both sexes," sitting about at the other end of the barn." Much drinking of liquor takes place. One of the men (who has made believe that he has been blind) rises and sings a song. It seems that "John Hobbs" at one time had been a member of the gang. Now that he has killed a man, he feels that he should rejoin his old companions. The leader of the gang is called "Ruffler." There are about twenty-five members of the gang. Several of the members stand up and show where their backs have been "crisscrossed with the ropy old welts left by the lash." One man has been branded with the letter "S" - indicating that he is a slave. Edward announces that he is King of England. The leader of the gang, Ruffler, helps protect Edward from "John Hobbs" (John Canty). Amused at the boy's insistence that he is King Edward, one of the gang suggests that the boy be called "Foo-foo the First, king of the Mooncalves." Edward is crowned with a tin basin, robed in a tattered blanket, throned upon a barrel, and sceptered with the tinker's soldering-iron. The tinker pretends to kiss the foot of "Foot-foo."

CHAPTER 18: THE PRINCE WITH THE TRAMPS

In the morning the vagabonds start on their march. "Jack" (the young king) is placed in the charge of Hugo, the boy who originally brought him from the inn. As the ruffians travel across the countryside, they invade a farmhouse and force the farmer and his helpers to prepare breakfast for them. On the edge of a village the gang splits up, so that each member may follow his own game. The king goes with Hugo, who plans to beg. When a stranger is halted by the groans of Hugo, the king warns the stranger away. Hugo quickly disappears, and the king flees in a different direction. The hungry young lad wanders through the forest. He finds and enters a barn. He makes himself a bed out of some horse blankets. In the middle of the night, he feels something touch him. Frightened, three times he extends his hand toward the unknown object. Eventually, he discovers that he is sleeping near a calf. The lonesome young traveler, delighted to have the calf's company, rearranges his blankets and cuddles himself up to the calf's back. Then he draws the covers up over himself and his "friends." Edward the Sixth has escaped his persecutors; he has companionship; he is warm; he is happy.

CHAPTER 19: THE PRINCE WITH THE PEASANTS

In the morning, King Edward finds that a wet rat had made itself a cozy bed on his chest. When Edward awakens, the rat scampers away. Soon, two little girls. Marjery and Prissy, come in and stare at Edward. When Edward tells them that he is the "King of England," the believe him for, as Marjery says, "Would he say a lie?" The mother of the children sympathizes with the king. She does not believe that he is a member of royalty, so she thinks up ways of surprising him into betraying his real identity. The only clue she has to his background is that the he knows a great deal about good food. She leaves him to "mind the cooking," and Edward compares himself to King Alfred, who burned the cottage cakes many years before. The food is burned, but the housewife feeds the boy. To pay for his meal, the lad is instructed to wash up the dishes, and then he is told to help the little girls who are paring winter apples. When the lad is given a basket of kittens to drown, he feels that he must "resign" from his position as helper. Suddenly, he sees John Canty and Hugo approaching the cottage, so he takes the kittens and steps out of the house by the back door. Leaving the small animals back of the house, he hurries away.

CHAPTER 20: THE PRINCE AND THE HERMIT

Just before Edward gains the shelter of the forest, he looks back and sees John Canty and Hugo in the distance. He makes his way quickly into the woods. Soon he becomes chilled. He does not want to spend the night in the woods without a shelter, so he is pleased when he sees the glimmer of a light in a small hut. Through the window of the little building he watches an aged man praying before a shrine. Near the man, on an old wooden box is an open book and a human skull. The man, whose frame is large and bony and whose hair and whiskers are very long and snowy white, is dressed in a robe of sheep skins. Edward recognizes the man as a holy hermit. The lad announces himself as the king. The hermit welcomes him, telling him that he shall "be at peace here." The boy is told that he may pray, read the Bible, and whip himself daily. He may wear a hair shirt and drink water. Edward tries to tell his story but the hermit mutters to himself and does not listen. The old man whispers into the king's ear: "I am an archangel!" Edward says to himself that he wishes he were with the outlaws again, for now he is the prisoner of a madman. The hermit explains to the boy that he was "made an archangel on this very spot ... five years ago, by angels sent from heaven." He claims that his religious house, meaning his monastery, was dissolved by Henry VIII. He has been "cast homeless upon the world." He keeps repeating that he might have been Pope. After a while, the old man becomes gentle and doctors Edward's bruises. The lad is put to bed, in a small adjoining room. While the young king sleeps, the hermit sits by the fire and sharpens a knife. It is evident that he is preparing to kill the young king. Edward stirs in his sleep. Finally, the hermit, gently and silently, ties the king's ankles together without awakening him. Next, the wrists are tied. Finally, a bandage is placed over the boy's head.

CHAPTER 21: HENDON TO THE RESCUE

Eventually the old man approaches Edward and sees that his eyes are open. The boy stares up at the knife in frozen horror. He struggles to release himself from his bonds, but he does not succeed. Edward cries. As the hermit bends over the young king with his knife, there is a noise outside the cabin. Leaving the boy covered with a sheepskin, the "archangel" goes outside and talks with Miles Hendon. Miles explains that he has just driven away John Canty and Hugo. He now wants to know where his young friend is. The old man claims that he has sent him on an errand. Edward tries to make some sort of a noise. The noise he makes resembles the sound of the wind. At the old man's suggestion, the two men finally ride away into the forest to search for Edward. Suddenly, Edward hears the door of the cabin open and in moments he is again the prisoner of John Canty and Hugo. The two ruffians hurry the lad away into the forest.

CHAPTER 22: A VICTIM OF TREACHERY

King Edward once again travels with the outlaws. Hugo amuses himself and the others with little meannesses to the king, such as stepping on Edward's toes. Finally, Edward reacts to Hugo's tormenting, and the king throws Hugo to the ground. Soon the two are in the midst of a circle of spectators. In very little time Edward completely subdues Hugo. Because of his victory Edward is now renamed "King of the Game-Cocks." Hugo plans to have vengeance on Edward. With the help of a tinker Hugo places a "clime" on Edward's leg. (A "clime" is an artificially created sore. To a passerby the sore resembles a hideous ulcer.) One of the friendly members of the gang appears and removes Edward's bandage. The head of the gang, Ruffler, decides that Edward should be promoted to the ranks of those who steal. Hugo plans a raid. Hugo and the king meet a woman who is carrying a fat package in a basket. Hugo snatches the woman's package and tosses the bundle into the king's hands. Then the avenging Hugo leaves. Edward throws the bundle on the ground and the woman seizes his hands and begins to scold him. Suddenly, a sword flashes in the air and Miles Hendon appears to rescue young Edward.

Comment (Chapters 17-22)

Compare the "gang" with the "gang" of robbers Huck and Jim find on the old river boat (in Huck Finn). Twain uses the word "stranger" for any unknown (or minor) character, such as the "benevolent stranger" in Chapter 18. When Edward escapes and applies at a farmhouse for food, he is turned away, for his clothes are against him. This is part of the "clothes philosophy" Twain borrows from Carlyle - that in the public eye clothes seem to designate one's social place. Another important aspect of the philosophy is that institutions, such as governments, need to be evaluated and readjusted, as do clothes. At the end of Chapter 18 there is a fine contrast between the cold outside world and the warm inside world (inside the barn). Chapter 19 presents an inquisitive woman who is reminiscent of Judith Loftus in *Huck Finn*. When Henry VIII severed the connection of the English church with Rome, he also abolished the monasteries. Evidently, the hermit had been a monk in one of these dissolved institutions. Chapter 21 in an unusually fine suspense sequence as Edward hopes, in vain, to be rescued. Note that the recaptured Edward has become popular with most of the vagabonds.

CHAPTER 23: THE PRINCE A PRISONER

Miles Hendon is pleased that Edward has addressed him as "Sir Miles." Edward is rebellious at being brought into a court, but Hendon reminds him that since he is "king" he should be willing to submit to the law. In court the judge is disturbed when he sees that the bundle had contained a plump little dressed pig. The punishment is death for anyone who steals a thing with a value of thirteen and one-half pennies. The pig is valued at more than three times this amount. The good woman does not wish to have the lad killed, and so she changes the amount of the value she has set on the pig. She lowers the value of eight pennies. An officer follows the woman out of the court and insists on buying the pig for eight pennies. Then, the king is given a lecture and sentenced to a short time in the common jail to be followed by public flogging. Edward starts to object, but Miles asks the lad to trust him.

CHAPTER 24: THE ESCAPE

On the way to the jail, Miles informs the officers with them that he witnessed the officer's buying the pig for eight pennies. Miles threatens to tell the judge unless the constable allows the two prisoners to escape. Also, Miles forces the man to promise to restore the pig to the woman whom he cheated.

CHAPTER 25: HENDON HALL

The two friends are on their way toward Hendon Hall. They travel for about ten miles and then they spend the night at a good inn. For several days they travel across the country. Miles tells Edward about his admirable father and his equally fine brother Arthur. He talks lovingly of Edith. Finally, the two travelers approach the village. Miles, excitedly, points out the towers of Hendon Hall. He promises to show the young king what state and grandeur are. Miles is proud of Hendon Hill, which has seventy rooms and twenty-seven servants. Soon the two pass the church and the local inn, The Red Lion. Finally, after a walk of a half-mile beyond an imposing gateway, they are in front of a noble mansion. Inside the building Miles sees his brother, Hugh, and he speaks excitedly to him. The brother makes believe that he does not know who Miles is. Hugh Hendon speaks of a letter which arrived from overseas six or seven years ago at Hendon Hall, informing the family that Miles had died in battle. Miles is shocked to learn that both his father and his brother Arthur are dead. He learns that the Lady Edith is living. Soon a beautiful lady, richly clothed, the Lady Edith, comes into the chamber. After staring for a long time into Miles' face she says: "I know him not!" Miles learns that the Lady Edith has become the wife of his brother Hugh. Miles springs at his brother and almost suffocates him. The servants are sent to get help. Miles states that he will remain where he is, for he is "master of Hendon Hall and all its belongings." (At the death of his father, Miles, by right, should have inherited Hendon Hall.)

CHAPTER 26: DISOWNED

Miles Hendon and the king wait for Hugh Hendon to bring the officers of the law. Edward wonders why the king is not missed in London. The lad writes a note, putting it in three tongues- Latin, Greek, and English. He gives the paper to Miles who absent-mindedly puts it in his pocket. He is preoccupied with his hurt over the thought that the Lady Edith has not indicated that she recognizes him. Suddenly, Lady Edith appears and warns him to leave immediately. She tells him that whether he is a mad imposter or whether he is the real Miles Hendon, Hugh Hendon will destroy him. She describes Hugh as a tyrant and speaks of herself as "a fettered slave." She tries to give Miles a purse of money. He refuses the gift. Suddenly officers come into the room. After a struggle, Miles and the king are bound and led to prison.

CHAPTER 27: IN PRISON

The king and Miles are chained in a large room of the prison. They are among about twenty other prisoners, both men and women. Miles puzzles over the actions of Lady Edith. For a week the king and Miles endure the noise of the prison. To while away the time, the prisoners fight, shout, and sing songs. One day, an old man is brought to see Miles. His name is Blake Andrews, and he was a servant for the Hendon family. The old man looks at Miles and says: "This is no Hendon - nor ever was!" After the jailer leaves the old man falls to his knees and, in a whisper, tells Miles that he recognizes him. In fact, he says: "I knew thee the moment I saw thee." A number of times each day the old servant visits Miles and the king, using the excuse that he wants to abuse the imposter (Miles). The daily visitor explains to Miles what has happened. Arthur, Miles' older brother, died. A letter was received saying that Miles was dead. Hugh insisted that he be allowed to marry Lady Edith. After the father died Hugh inherited the estate. It has been said that Lady Edith has found evidence that Hugh, himself, wrote the letter about Miles' death. Many tales are told of the cruelty of Hugh to his wife and the servants. Blake Andrews then gives the news that Henry VIII is to be buried within several days. He adds that the new king will be crowned at Westminster the twentieth of the month. Blake speaks of the popularity of the new king, Edward the Sixth. The real King Edward is struck dumb with amazement. He wonders if the person on the throne might be the beggar boy he left dressed in his own garments in the palace. In the prison two women are very kind to the king. They are imprisoned because they are Baptist. One day, all the prisoners are marched to the courtyard where they stare at the two women, chained to posts in the middle of the square. A crowd of people come to watch the punishment. The two women are burned at the stake. The king is very unhappy when he sees the suffering of his two friends. Many people in the jail talk with Edward, and he becomes convinced that they have not been treated justly.

CHAPTER 28: THE SACRIFICE

The time of the trial for Miles arrives. He is sentenced to sit two hours in the pillory. The king is let off with a lecture and a warning. An egg is thrown at Miles' cheek. The king starts to speak out, ordering that Miles be set free. The officer mentions the possibility of whipping the youngster. Sir Hugh suggests that the boy should receive six lashes. Miles says: "Let him go - I will take his lashes." Sir Hugh then declares that Miles should have twelve strokes of the whip. Edward inwardly suffers as he watches his friend during the whipping. When it is over, the king takes up the whip from the ground and touching Miles' bleeding shoulders lightly with it, whispers that now Miles is an earl.

CHAPTER 29: TO LONDON

After being released from the stocks Miles decides that he should go to London and ask the young king to help him. He remembers that one of his father's friends, Sir Humphrey Marlow, might be able to help him. Politely, Miles asks Edward where they should go. The man is pleased when the boy says: "To London!" As the two travelers walk across London Bridge, on the day before Coronation Day, they become hopelessly separated from each other.

Comment (Chapters 23-29)

Miles Hendon's speculations on his own place as a "specter-knight" in Edward's "Kingdom of Dreams and Shadows" is very reminiscent of Cervantes' *Don Quixote*. Miles' quick-witted talk to the constable is the basis of a humorous **episode** comparable to the one in which Tom Sawyer talks his friends into white-washing a fence for him (in *Tom Sawyer*). While Edward and Miles travel toward Hendon Hall, Miles tells, in flashback, of his adventures since the boy was lured from his protection. Edward almost enjoys Miles' distress at not being recognized, for now he feels Miles will understand how unhappy one feels not to be recognized as himself. Miles is identified as "the murderous stranger" by Hugh, his brother. In Chapter 29, Miles-a man of action-needs "something to turn his energies to, a distinctly defined object to accomplish." It is a keynote to his character.

CHAPTER 30: TOM'S PROGRESS

Meanwhile, Tom Canty, masquerading as King Edward the Sixth, has decided that being king does have a bright side. He has lost his fears. No longer is he embarrassed in the presence of the courtiers. With great ease he orders Lady Elizabeth and Lady Jane Grey into his presence, when he wishes to play or talk. He is not upset when these lofty personages kiss his hand at parting. He doubles the number of his gentlemen-at-arms, who accompany him to dinner. He likes his splendid clothes - and even orders more. He decides that four hundred servants are two few for his proper grandeur, so he increases the number to twelve hundred servants. He makes war upon unjust laws. At first he has painful thoughts about the lost prince, but in time thoughts of the real Edward fade out of his mind. Tom is able to forget his mother and sisters. On the night of the nineteenth of February, the day before King Edward the Sixth is to be solemnly crowned, happy Tom Canty goes to bed, surrounded by the pomps of royalty. At the very same time, Edward, the true king, stands outside Westminster Abbey watching the workmen.

CHAPTER 31: THE RECOGNITION PROC SS

On the morning of Coronation Day, Tom Canty is splendidly dressed. He is the most important figure in a procession which begins at the Tower of London. Tom is thrilled when he sees two of his ragged Offal Court comrades. How happy it would make him to tell these two cheering youngsters that they are exercising their lungs to praise him-Tom Canty. Occasionally, Tom scatters bright new coins for the crowd. Suddenly Tom sees his mother on the edge of the crowd. Up flies his hand, palm outward, before his eyes. Tom's mother recognizes him and forces her way past the guards. She cries out: "Oh my child, my darling!; Tom says: "I do not know this woman!" From this time on Tom Canty's heart is filled with remorse. He becomes thoughtful. He looks sad. The Lord Protector rides to his side and reminds him to smile upon the people. Tom does smile, but he is not happy. Again the Lord Protector reminds him that the eyes of the world are upon him. Tom then says that the woman who approached him in the procession is his mother. The Lord Protector thinks that the lad has gone mad again.

CHAPTER 32: CORONATION DAY

Early on Coronation Day, the galleries are filled with people. At seven o'clock in the morning the peeresses of the realm start arriving. They are decorated with diamonds. Then the foreign ambassadors arrive. Finally the sound of artillery announces that the king and his grand procession have arrived. The nobles of the realm are seated. The heads of the church take their places. Then Tom Canty, clothed in a long robe of cloth-of-gold, steps forth. The choir sings. The Archbishop of Canterbury holds the crown of England over the trembling mock king's head. Suddenly, a boy, bareheaded and clothed in coarse garments, walks up the great center aisle. He raises his hand and says: "I forbid you to set the crown of England upon that forfeited head. I am the king." Tom Canty cries out: "He is the king!" The Protector thinks that the "king" has lost his mind. Tom Canty rushes forward and falls upon his knees before the real king saying: "Put on thy crown and enter thine own again!" The Lord Protector is puzzled. He begins to ask the real king questions. The Protector declares that the answers to the questions about the royal family are correct-but the "king" (Tom Canty) could offer the same correct answers. Suddenly the Protector remembers that no one knows where the Great Seal is. The true king describes a certain hidden closet in the palace. Lord St. John leaves to investigate this closet, to see whether or not the Great Seal of England is in it. While this noble is gone, the people who have been surrounding Tom Canty gradually begin to cluster around the true king. When Lord St. John returns, he says: "The Seal is not there!" The crowd around the true king quietly melts back to its original position around Tom Canty. The Lord Protector calls out that the imposter (the real Edward) should be whipped through the streets of the town. Tom Canty then tries to make Edward remember all the details of their first meeting. Edward suddenly remembers that he placed the Great Seal "in an arm-piece of the Milanese armor that hangs on the wall." This was done hurriedly, when the excited lad rushed out of the room to reprimand the soldier who hurt Tom Canty's hand. Lord St. John goes to the palace and eventually returns carrying with him the Great Seal of England. The people send up shouts of praise for the "true king." The Lord Protector orders that Tom Canty be stripped and flung into the Tower. Edward says that this will not be. Then Tom admits that he has been using the Great Seal of England to crack nuts with. The coronation now continues with the true king in his rightful place.

CHAPTER 33: EDWARD AS KING

All this time Miles Hendon has been hunting for his little friend, Edward. Weary, he takes a nap beside a hedge in the country. When he approaches the palace, on the day after the coronation, he meets Edward's whipping boy, who recognizes Miles as the person the king is seeking. The whipping boy turns out to be the son of Sir Humphrey Marlowe, the close friend of Miles' father, Sir Richard Hendon. Miles accompanies the whipping boy to the palace and waits outside, while the boy goes to see His Majesty. Some officers find Miles and search him. They remove from Miles' pocket the letter that Edward wrote in three languages.

The letter is sent in to the king. Soon an officer ushers Miles into the splendid chamber of the king. Miles is about five steps away from the young king whose head is bent down and aside.

When the king raises his face, Miles Hendon recognizes his young friend. He wonders how he can prove whether or not the king is the small companion of his travels. An idea occurs to him. He gets a chair and sits himself in it-in the presence of the king. The king declares that it is Miles' right to sit in the presence of the King of England. Also, Edward declares that Miles is now a peer of England, Earl of Kent, and that he is to be given gold and land. Sir Hugh is discovered among the courtiers and the king orders him to be led away. Then, Tom Canty, quaintly but richly clothed, kneels before the king. Edward declares that from this day, Tom will live at Christ Hospital and that he shall be highly respected, for, at one time, Tom "hath been royal." Tom is to be given the title of "King's Ward."

Comment (Chapters 30-33 and "Conclusion")

Note that Tom at first dreams of being a prince; then he is a prince and felt himself a captive; finally, he adapts to his new situation and is happy with being king. Twain again seems to use the services of a "chronicler" whom he cites at length in the description of the coronation procession. In Chapter 31, notice that Tom's mood changes from one of joyousness to one of sorrowful remorse, after he refuses recognition to his mother. For variety, Twain uses the present tense for the first few pages of Chapter 32; the rest of the tale is told in the past tense. The "coigns of vantage" refers to the advantageous positions taken by members of the coronation audience. Note the brilliant description of the melting away of Tom Canty's following to the side of Edward, with the gradual change being compared to the slow "movement ... observed in a kaleidoscope." The coronation **episode** ends with a burst of humor, as Tom confesses that he has been using the Great Seal of England "to crack nuts with!" Perhaps coincidence is carried to considerable length as Miles Hendon is recognized by the whipping boy, who happens to be the son of the man he is seeking, Sir Humphrey Marlow. Miles cleverly sits in front of the sovereign to prove to himself whether or not Edward is the friend with whom he had traveled. The fact that John Canty is "never heard of again" allows Twain the privilege of not having to mete out imaginative justice to the father of one of his two heroes. Twain ends his tale rather gracefully, as he describes Tom Canty's long and honorable career as the "King's Ward" and Edward's brief, but compassionate, reign.

CONCLUSION

Justice And Retribution

And so the loose strings of the novel are tied neatly together. Miles Hendon is relieved to find out that the Lady Edith did recognize him. Her husband, Hugh, had made her promise not to recognize Miles-if she had acknowledged Miles, Hugh would have had Miles killed. Hugh goes to the continent of Europe, where he soon dies. Miles and the Lady Edith are married. Tom Canty's father is never heard of again. During King Edward's lifetime, he enjoys telling the story of his adventures. He likes to speak of mixing himself into a gang of hearty workmen and slipping into Westminster Abbey. Once in the Abbey he climbed on top of the tomb of Edward the Confessor. There he fell asleep - and almost did not awaken in time to claim his rights. Both Miles Hendon and Tom Canty are favorites of the king. Miles continues to claim the privilege of sitting in his monarch's presence. Tom Canty lives to be a very old man, honored and revered. The people remember that at one time he had been royal. He is known as the King's Ward. King Edward the Sixth lives only a few years. He remembers the lessons learned when he took the place of pauper. Knowing the need for mercy among his people, King Edward is always compassionate and merciful.

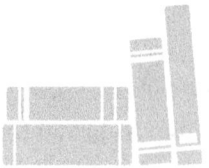

THE PRINCE AND THE PAUPER

CHARACTER ANALYSES

The Prince Of Wales

As drawn by Twain, Edward Tudor, Prince of Wales, has the attributes which would have made him, had he lived long enough, a just and merciful monarch. We see him angry at cruelty, as he rescues Tom Canty from the guard. Later on, in John Canty's home, Edward will not allow Mrs. Canty to take a beating for him; he cannot allow someone else to suffer in his stead. This has nothing to do with allowing his whipping boy to take his punishment. This is one of his royal perquisites. Edward is very conscious of his royal dignity. When he is pushed into the street in his rags, he tells the soldier that his own person is sacred and that the soldier will hang for this impertinence. He treats Miles Hendon, his protector, like a palace servant. Miles describes him as a bold-tongued little rascal who is soldier-like in his defiance of a rude mob. At the end of Chapter 22, he haughtily commands Miles Hendon to carve the rabble to rags.

Again showing a princely trait, Edward is curious about his people, eager to learn and observe. He is fascinated by Tom's stories of life in the slums, although Edward sees it as a life of freedom. He is adventurous enough to change clothes with Tom. He has known only his finery, his silks and satins, his jeweled sword, his fine buskins and feathered cap. He does not feel degraded by putting on the clothes of the pauper. Edward's dignity does not depend on his outer aspect, his clothes, but on his inbred feelings about himself as a person. It is not he, but others, who fail to appreciate him at his personal worth, and judge him by what he wears. Once he puts on the clothes of the pauper, everybody accepts him as the pauper; only he is never confused, always knowing who and what he is. Once he is inside the pauper's skin, so to speak, by wearing Tom's rags, he is quick to learn what life is like for the poor of his kingdom, and to resolve to do something about the injustice and misery he sees. In his own way, he is democratic; that is, he accepts people at their human value. He does not laugh at Tom's rude table manners, but sends away the servants so that Tom will not be embarrassed by them. When the farm woman is kind to him and feeds him, he allows the family to sit with him. Although he expects Miles Hendon to serve him, he rewards im for his loyalty and courage, and keeps every promise he made him. He is resourceful, as is shown by his finding a way to get into Westminster Abbey in time to claim the coronation which is rightfully his. Finally, he is forgiving, saving Tom from the fate which ordinarily might be meted out to an imposter, and placing the boy under his protection.

Tom Canty

In one sense, Tom Canty personifies Twain's belief that every man could be a king. Even in his miserable existence, he dreams of royal splendors. He imagines that he is a prince, and organizes a royal court of his own. In his imagination, he lives the life which he ascribes to royalty. He is ambitious enough to take advantage of Father Andrew's teaching, and learns as much as he can from the priest. When he comes to the actuality of living the princely life, he finds there are difficulties he had not dreamed of, and at first is timid and shy, wanting only to get out of the trap in which he finds himself. But again, he has the desire to learn, and learn he does from every source: the supposed sister, Princess Elizabeth and the supposed cousin, Lady Jane Grey; his whipping boy; books on etiquette; the nobles and servants with whom he is surrounded. He takes on kingly virtues. He enjoys being able to dispense mercy to accused criminals. He begins to understand some of the responsibilities of being a king. But he also develops other qualities of the kingly estate. He begins to confuse himself with his role. He likes to hear the call, "Way for the king!" He forgets about his family and about the real Edward Tudor. The corruption reaches its **climax** when he sees his mother in the crowd and flings up his hand in fear. The fear is that he will be dragged back to his former unsavory existence. It is both the fear and the corruption he has undergone that make him say to her, "I do no know you, woman!" If he had become completely hardened, he would have kept up the masquerade, and kept his place, at no matter what cost to anyone else. But he has innate courage and honor. When the real Edward appears in Westminster Abbey, and declares himself the king, Tom says, "He is the king!" Even this declaration would not have decided the issue, since Tom for some time had been declaring he was not Edward Tudor. But Tom went to the length of helping Edward prove his kingship by ferreting out the Great Seal of England. Tom's honesty and integrity proved him as good as any king. He didn't need the royal trappings of which he had once dreamed. As Twain put it, his was "an honorable history."

Miles Hendon

If *The Prince and the Pauper* can be said to have a hero, Miles Hendon is he. He has many outstanding qualities. He is intelligent, resourceful, courageous, kind, compassionate and full of humor. As in the case of Tom and Edward, his status is indicated by his costume: his doublet and trunks are of rich material, but faded and threadbare; their gold-lace adornments are sadly tarnished; his ruff is rumpled and damaged; the plume in his hat is broken and has a ragged and disreputable look. He wears a long rapier in a rusty iron sheath. We know at once from his appearance that he is of high birth but fallen through some mischance to his present lowly position. His misfortunes haven't changed his basic nature; he has not become bitter or mean or vengeful. He is constant in his affections. His goal is to get back to Hendon Hall and Lady Edith, with whom he had been in love before he left home. His faith takes a rude blow when he sees the people he cares about disowning him - not knowing, of course, it is only to protect him - but he still does not show any trace of cruelty.

Miles Hendon is basically a man of action, taking the fortunes of life as they come to him. Without reflection, he catches up Edward in his arms and decides to protect him. He says to John Canty, "Go thy ways, and set quick about it, for I like not much bandying of words, being not overpatient in my nature." His attitude to the boy-to anything helpless and in need of care - is summed up in his vow: "I will be his friend ... I will be his elder brother and care for him and watch over him."

His wit is basically that of a man of action. In Chapter 23, he uses nonsense Latin quotations to persuade the constable to look the other way. In Chapter 24, he uses his wit to get some rest, when requesting permission to sit in Edward's presence, during their wanderings. He shows both wit and daring in sitting in the King's presence, to determine whether or not that is his friend on the throne.

Miles Hendon has been himself during his exile and his sojourn among the poor. He is himself when he comes into his own, when his lands come back to him and he is given further awards by the king. He is the man of whom Kipling wrote, who could "walk with Kings, nor lose the common touch."

THE PRINCE AND THE PAUPER

CRITICAL COMMENTARY

Since *The Prince and the Pauper* is one of Mark Twain's most popular and widely admired books about young people, any major criticism of his work must have reference to this famous tale of sixteenth-century England. The following brief summary of criticism is subdivided into three parts: (1) Mark Twain biography, letters, and bibliography; (2) collected works and specialized editions; and (3) critical commentary of Mark Twain and his works.

MARK TWAIN BIOGRAPHY, LETTERS, AND BIBLIOGRAPHY

Twain himself provides much material for study in three volumes by A.B. Paine, entitled *Mark Twain, A Biography* (1912). This early, affirmative picture of Twain is for the general reader, not the thorough scholar. In 1920, Van Wyck Brooks's *The Ordeal of Mark Twain* tries to prove that Twain is thwarted in his literary development, not only by his Missouri background, but also by his later Victorian and wealthy friends in the East. Bernard De Voto in *Mark Twain's America* (1932) attacks the Brooks thesis and claims that Twain's development was greatly enhanced by his frontier background. Edward Wagenknecht, in *Mark Twain: The Man and His Work* (1935, 1961), argues for the view that Twain's works reflect his frontier background and his own attitudes toward life. In 1943, DeLancey Ferguson, in *Mark Twain: Man and Legend*, stresses the environmental and literary influences which helped to form Twain into a prominent literary figure. Dixon Wecter's *Sam Clemens of Hannibal* (1952) emphasizes the part played in Twain's development by his home town, Hannibal, Missouri. Kenneth Andrew's 1950 book, *Nook Farm: Mark Twain's Hartford Circle*, pictures the influences of the East on Twain, who, late in life, yearned for the simplicity of his early Mississippi River Valley days. A relatively late work which helps broaden one's view of Twain the person is Caroline T. Harnsberger's *Mark Twain: Family Man* (1960). Jerry Allen's *The Adventures of Mark Twain* (1954) is a very readable biography. Frank Baldanza's *Mark Twain: An Introduction and Interpretation* (1961) offers a good introductory picture of the most celebrated author of the Mississippi River Valley.

Mark Twain's letters throw light on him as a person and as a developing literary artist. Among the collections of letters available is A. B. Paine's two-volume edition of *Letters, Arranged with Comment* (1917), as well as Dixon Wecter's two editions, *Mark Twain to Mrs. Fairbanks* (1949) and *The Love Letters of Mark Twain* (1949). Some other sources of letters are: Ivan Benson's *Mark Twain: Business Man* (1946); G. E. Dane's edition of *Letters from the Sandwich Islands* (1937, 1938); Thomas Nickerson's collection, *Letters from Honolulu* (1939); Cyril Clemens's *Republican Letters* (1941); E. M. Branch's edition, *Letters in the Muscatina Journal* (1942); E. E. Leisy's collection, *The Letters of Quintus Curtius Snodgrass* (1946); Theodore Hornberger's edition, *Mark Twain's Letters to Will Bowen*

(1941); and "Mark Twain's Letters in the San Francisco Call" (Twainian, 1949, 1952).

Mark Twain bibliography is found in numerous places. Of primary importance is Merle Johnson's *A Bibliography of the Works of Mark Twain, Samuel Langhorne Clemens* (1935). Of value is the alphabetical listing in Lewis Leary's *Articles on American Literature*, 1900-1950 (1954). A splendidly workable edition of references to Mark Twain in Harry Hayden Clark's "Mark Twain," in *Eight American Authors*, ed., Floyd Stovall (1956). Consult the 1963 "Bibliographical Supplement" by J. Chesley Mathews for additional references.

COLLECTED WORKS AND SPECIALIZED EDITIONS

Four collected are available: *The Writings of Mark Twain*, edited by A. B. Paine, 37 volumes (1922-1925); the *Author's National Edition of The Writings of Mark Twain*, 25 volumes (1901-1907); and *Mark Twain's Works*, 23 volumes (1933). Many of Twain's letters and speeches are included in collections of periodicals. See Lewis Leary's *Articles on American Literature*, 1900-1950, as well as Harry Hayden Clark's "Mark Twain," *Eight American Authors*. Charles Neider has published in several volumes a number of the short Mark Twain selections. Special collections of Mark Twain manuscripts are found in the following places: the Berg Collection of the New York Public Library; the William Dean Howells Papers at Harvard; the Boston Public Library; the Huntington Library; the Princeton Library; and the Library of Congress. H. N. Smith, of the University of California, has in his charge numerous unpublished manuscripts, the property of the Mark Twain estate.

CRITICAL COMMENTARY ON MARK TWAIN AND HIS WORKS

Much has been written on Twain, both the man and the works. First, consider influences and sources. In 1937, Walter Blair places Twain within the general tradition of Native American Humor. See, also, Constance Rourke's *American Humor*, 1931, concerning the elements of folklore in Twain's works, R. W. Frantz's "The Role of Folklore in *Huckleberry Finn*," *American Literature* (1956), and R. E. Bell's "How Mark Twain Comments on Society through Use of Folklore," *Mark Twain Quarterly* (1955), Earlier, in 1934, Minnie M. Brashear wrote of the part Twain's Hannibal, Missouri, background played in his literary development, as well as the influence on him of eighteenth-century writers, such as Swift and Thomas Paine (*Mark Twain: Son of Missouri*). G. A. Cardwell's *Twins of Genius* (1953) contains the thirty-eight letters exchanged between Mark Twain and his influential literary friend, George Washington Cable. See, also, the following two thoughtful articles: P. J. Carter's "The Influence of the Nevada Frontier on Mark Twain," *Western Humanities Review* (1959) and Henry Nash Smith's "Mark Twain's Images of Hannibal: From St. Petersburg to Eseldorf," *University of Texas Studies in English* (1958).

Much of Twain's work is concerned with the question of man's ethical conduct. To some extent, Gladys C. Bellamy discusses this aspect of Mark Twain in her book, *Mark Twain As a Literary Artist* (1950). Three articles review some portions of Twain's ethical attitudes: H. H. Waggoner's "Science in the Thought of Mark Twain," American Literature (1937); R. T. Oliver's "Mark Twain and Religion," Christian Leader (1940); and F. C. Flower's "Mark Twain's Theories of Morality," *Mark Twain Quarterly* (1948). See, also, the two following studies: G. M. Rubenstein's "The Moral Structure of Huckleberry *Finn*,"

College English (1956) and A. E. Jones's "Mark Twain and the Determinism of What Is Man?" *American Literature* (1957).

Readers of *The Prince and the Pauper* and *A Connecticut Yankee in King Arthur's Court* are keenly aware of Mark Twain's strong political and social points of view. V. L. Parrington's *Main Currents in American Thought* (Volume III) (1930) underlines Twain's attack on monarchy and the established church. See, also, A. L. Scott's "Mark Twain Looks at Europe," *South Atlantic Quarterly* (1953). Concerning the Civil War and Twain, at least three articles have been written: John Gerber's "Mark Twain's 'Private Campaign, '" Civil War History (1955); F. W. Lorch's "Mark Twain and the 'Campaign that Failed, '" *American Literature* (1941); and G. H. Orian's "Walter Scott, Mark Twain, and the Civil War," *South Atlantic Quarterly* (1941). Some other studies, emphasizing Mark Twain's political and social feelings, are: Paul Carter's "The Influence of W. D. Howells upon Mark Twain's Social Satire," *University of Colorado Studies* (1953); A. L. Scott's "Mark Twain: Critic of Conquest," *Dalhousie Review* (1955); F. R. Leavis's "The Americanness of American Literature," Commentary (1952); and Earl Hilton's "Mark Twain's Theory of History," *Papers of the Michigan Academy of Science, Art, and Letters* (1951, 1952). Two relatively recent books and two articles should be of value of the reader of Mark Twain with an interest in his political-social activities: P. S. Foner's *Mark Twain: Social Critic* (1958); R. B. Solomon's *Twain and the Image of History* (1961); P. J. Carter's "Mark Twain and the American Labor Movement," *New England Quarterly* (1957); and Sherwood Cummings's "Mark Twain's Social Darwinism," *Huntington Library Quarterly* (1957).

Mark Twain's ideas on literary composition and his general point of view concerning aesthetics are scattered throughout the works. Once in a while, Twain wrote essays on literature as such; for example. "How to Tell a Story" And "Is Shakespeare Dead?" Besides Gladys C. Bellamy's excellent book, *Mark Twain as a Literary Artist* (1950), and the index to the comprehensive *Transitions in American Literary History*, ed., Harry Hayden Clark (1953), there are numerous other aids toward understanding Twain's individualized approach to fiction. Some of the outstanding articles are: Brander Matthews's "Mark Twain and the Art of Writing," *Harper's* (1920); S. B. Liljegren's "The Revolt Against Romanticism in American Literature as Evidenced in the Works of S. L. Clemens," *Studia Neophilologica* (1945); G. W. Feinstein's "Mark Twain's Idea of Story Structure," *American Literature* (1946); E. H. Goold's "Mark Twain on the Writing of Fiction," American Literature (1954); R. A. Wiggins's "Mark Twain and the Drama," *American Literature* (1953); Harry Hayden Clark's "The Influence of Science on American Literary Criticism 1860-1910, Including the Vogue of Taine," *Transactions of the Wisconsin Academy of Sciences, Arts, and Letters* (1955); Pascal Covici's *Mark Twain's Humor: The Image of a World* (1962); F. R. Roger's *Mark Twain's* **Burlesque** *Patterns: As Seen in the Novels and Narratives 1855-1885* (1960); H. N. Smith's *Mark Twain: The Development of Writer* (1962); Sherwood Cummings's "Science and Mark Twain's Theory of Fiction," *Philological Quarterly* (1958); Otto Friedrich's "Mark Twain and the Nature of Humor," *Discourse* (1959); J. C. Gerber's "The Relation between Point of View and style, in the Works of Mark Twain," in *Style in Prose Fiction: English Institute Essays* (1958), ed., H. C. Martin; J. B. Hoben's "Mark Twain: On the Writer's Use of Language," *American Scholar* (1956); and S. J. Krause's "Twain's Method and Theory of Composition," *Modern Philology* (1959). Numerous studies of Twain's language have been made, some of the most important being: F. G. Emberson's "Mark Twain's Vocabulary: A General Survey," *University of Missouri Studies* (1935); R. L. Ramsay and F. G. Emberson's "A Mark Twain Lexicon," "University of Missouri Studies (1938); Katherine Buxbaum's "Mark Twain and American

Dialect," *American Speech* (1927); C. J. Lowell's "The Background of Mark Twain's Vocabulary," *American Speech* (1947); and H. L. Mencken's monumental *American Language* (1930). Among the histories of American fiction which deal with Mark Twain, five might be mentioned: A. H. Quinn's *American Fiction* (1936); W. F. Taylor's *A History of American Letters* (1936); Carl Van Doren's *The American Novel: 1789-1939* (1940) Alexander Cowie's *The Rise of the American Novel* (1948); and Edward Wagenknecht's *Cavalcade of the American Novel* (1952). Prominent among the histories of American literature are three works which discuss Twain: "The Cambridge History of American Literature" (essay by S. P. Sherman) (1921); V. L. Parrington's *Main Currents in American Thought* (Volume 3) (1930); and "A Literary History of the United States" (essay by Dixon Wecter) (1948). For comprehensive annotations concerning studies of *Huckleberry Finn* see Harry Hayden Clark's "Mark Twain," *Eight American Authors* (1963 edition), pp. 347-355. For a discussion of other individual works of Mark Twain, see, also, H. H. Clark's section on Twain in *Eight American Authors*, pp. 355-361. For those who find of interest Frank Luther Mott's comments on Mark Twain in *Golden Multitudes: The Story of Best Sellers in the United States* (1947), reference might be made to Roger Asselinean's "The Literary Reputation of Mark Twain from 1910 to 1950: A Critical Essay and a Bibliography" (1954).

Two helpful collections of essays about Mark Twain and his works are: Henry Nash Smith, ed., *Mark Twain: A Collection of Critical Essays* (Twentieth Century Views Series) (1963) and Guy A. Cardwell, ed., *Discussions of Mark Twain* (Discussions of Literature Series) (1963). Lewis Leary's *Mark Twain* (University of Minnesota Pamphlets on American Writers) (1960) is a good general introduction. (See, also, Lewis Leary's edition, *A Casebook on Mark Twain's Wound*, 1962.) E. H. Long's *Mark Twain Handbook* (1958) is worthwhile for the broad scope of coverage of Twain material.

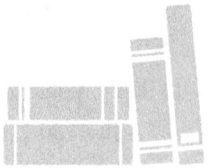

THE PRINCE AND THE PAUPER

ESSAY QUESTIONS AND ANSWERS

Question: Discuss Mark Twain's use of **similes** and metaphors. (A simile is a figure of speech in which one thing is likened to another, dissimilar thing. A **metaphor** is a figure of speech in which one thing is spoken of as if it were another.)

Answer: In Chapter 11, many a "slender spire" of a London church rises "into the sky, incrusted with sparkling lights." The spires seem "like jeweled lances thrust aloft." This **simile** uses an image appropriate to the times, a lance being used in battle (possibly mostly for display purposes in the early sixteenth century). In Chapter 18, just before the king enters the barn, he is startled by the "soft rustling of the dry leaves overhead, so like human whispers" they seem to sound. The fleeing king is trying to escape his pursuers (John Canty and Hugo) and a "sound" like a human voice is enough to frighten him. In Chapter 21, the hermit sharpens his knife, preparatory to killing Edward. In "his aspect and attitude," he resembles "nothing so much as a grizzly, monstrous spider, gloating over some hopeless insect" that is "bound and helpless in his web." The old man, bent over, maneuvering about his cottage, probably looks like a spider. In Chapter 31, the "shining pageant" winds "like a radiant and interminable serpent down the crooked lanes of the quaint old city." (There seems little connection of "serpent" with the tale-unless Tom Canty should feel guilty or snake-like because he has taken another boy's throne.) Moments later, the crowds shout: "Long live Edward of England!" Tom hears it "only as one hears the thunder of the surf when it is blown to the ear out of a great distance." (Twain likes to refer to water images.) Tom remembers how he said to his mother, "I do not know you, woman." The woman resounds against the "king's soul" as the "strokes of a funeral bell" resound "upon the soul of a surviving friend when they remind him of secret treacheries suffered at his hands by him that is gone." The somber, funeral quality suggested by the bell symbolizes Tom's secret remorse because he has been very unkind to his mother. A splendid image is projected when Twain describes the "movement" of courtiers from Tom's side to Edward's side, during the coronation in Westminster Abbey. The movement is such as observed in a kaleidoscope and makes an exact parallel to the gorgeous display of pageantry. The change of the colors is well compared to the movement of the courtiers. Twain uses a number of striking similes. There is only one **metaphor** of importance. In Chapter 16, Tom Canty (attempting to adjust himself to his new role as king) is called a "poor little ash-cat," now somewhat more accustomed "to his strange garret" than previously.

Question: *Huckleberry Finn* and *The Prince and the Pauper* are both about young boys, yet *The Prince and the Pauper* is considered more a book for children than is *Huckleberry Finn*. Why should this be true?

Answer: In *The Prince and the Pauper*, Mark Twain puts down everything exactly as he wishes the reader to see it; in *Huckleberry Finn*, he draws situations in which the characters seem to be doing and saying one thing, but the reader knows perfectly well that something else is meant. The reader is free to exercise his imagination and intelligence and make his own discoveries as to motives and meaning. For instance, Huck is brought up to believe that helping a runaway slave is immoral and sinful. After helping Jim, his conscience prompts him to write a letter to Jim's owner, telling her where her slave Jim is to be found. After writing the letter, he says: "I felt good and all washed clean of sin for the first time I had ever felt so in my life, and I knowed I could pray now. But I didn't do it straight off but laid the paper down and set there thinking - thinking how good it was all this had happened so, and how near I come to being lost and going to hell." This is Twain in his best satiric mood, presenting the mores of his time exactly as "good" people accepted them, but leaving it to the reader to interpret the real meaning. In the book, Huck goes on thinking about his friend Jim, how good Jim had been to him, and realizes he can't betray a friend. He tears up the letter, saying, "All right, then, I'll go to hell." Huck thinks of himself and pictures himself as being evil. We know that Huck is good. But Twain lets us figure this out for ourselves.

In *The Prince and the Pauper*, young Edward Tudor is exposed to the miseries of the people of his kingdom, which Twain describes in detail. "The king was furious over these inhumanities and wanted Hendon to break jail and fly with him to Westminster so that he could mount his throne and hold out his scepter in mercy over these unfortunate people and save their lives." There is no indirection here. Twain says exactly what he means. He has Edward speak directly: "... the laws that have dishonored thee [the lawyer in prison] and shamed the English name shall be swept from the statute books. The world is made wrong; kings should go to school to their own laws at times, and so learn mercy." Edward is good, he is presented as good, and the reader doesn't have to figure out anything for himself.

The narrative style also plays a part in differentiating the two books. Huck Finn tells his story from his own point of view, which means the reader sees the happenings from two angles: Huck's subjective reaction to what is happening, and what the reader knows, reasonably, is really happening. In *The Prince and the Pauper* everything is described by the author exactly as he wants us to see it. He tells the story in absolutely straightforward style.

Question: Did Mark Twain intend this story as an allegory or as real story? Did he take the situation seriously or was he using it to make a point?

Answer: Mark Twain was an idealist who dreamed of a world made perfect by the banishment of injustice and inhumanity. This is not the only book in which he attacked oppression, inequality and greed. The Gilded Age exposed corruption in high places. *The Prince and the Pauper* is completely taken up with dramatizing the misery created by misuse of power, by the cruelty of man to his fellow man, by blindness to the rights and feelings of others. Although the story was first shaped as a tale for his children, and, in fact, dedicated to his young daughters Susie and Clara, it is anything but a simple story. It is a social tract from beginning to end.

There is no evidence that young Edward Tudor at any time ever lived any life but a princely life. There have been many whispered rumors of royal disappearances and substitutions, e.g., the story of the lost Dauphin, the French prince who was supposed to have been saved from the guillotine during the French Revolution and spirited to America; the story of Anastasia, who was supposed to have been the youngest Romanov princess and saved from the massacre of her family during the Russian Revolution. There is even a story which has never been proved or disproved about Edward's half-sister, Elizabeth I, who was alleged to have died as a young girl, with someone substituted for her to keep the power in the Tudor family. The only basis that Twain might have had for using Edward as a figure in his story was that Edward's short reign was, indeed, noted for its mercy in a time when monarchs generally used their power with a heavy hand. The fact, too, that Edward was really a boy king might have appealed to Twain, for it fitted neatly in with one of his favorite literary devices: boys who liked to play games of make-believe. It is from the make-believe of the two boys, when they change clothes for a moment to step into each other's identities, that the happenings of the story spring. Twain had other instances of mistaken identity, in "Pudd'nhead Wilson" and "Tom Sawyer, Detective."

Twain's preoccupation with changed identity, with an outward appearance which has nothing to do with the inner reality, may have reflected some of his own philosophy. He felt that many things in life which the society around him valued were a fraud. He disliked materialism and outer pretense. Yet he himself had his materialistic side. He gambled heavily on the success of the typesetting machine on which he eventually lost money. He went on lecture tours strictly to make money. He may have felt like two persons: one, the writer, dedicated to his art; the other, a fortune-seeker, strictly out to make money. This may account for his preoccupation with the **theme** of people who are not recognized for what they really are. For in Edward Tudor, Tom Canty, and Miles Hendon, he not only has people who, one way or another, become familiar with misery and injustice, but people who cannot make themselves be seen in their true identities. He repeated the situation with King Arthur's disguise in "Connecticut Yankee." In the last analysis, it might have been from his disguise which each man wears that Twain felt injustice rises, as it did to his three protagonists. The search for one's own true identity, stripped of the built-up disguises which are foisted on mankind by conventions, pretensions and learned ignorances, may well have been one of the preoccupations which Mark Twain-Samuel Clemens was exploring in *The Prince and The Pauper*. On whichever level the novel is taken, social tract or philosophical speculation, the people in it are seen as figures on which he can drape his beliefs.

Question: What parts of *The Prince and The Pauper* might be taken as really applying to Mark Twain's own time, and not to the sixteenth century?

Answer: Although Baptists certainly were not persecuted in Twain's time, the burning of the Baptists illustrated an evil prevalent in any age, religious intolerance. (Chapter 27.) Edward, as king, might have been expected to view the burning of "heretics" as justice; instead, in his agonized speech, he sums up the feelings of any humane person exposed to such senseless bigotry.

In Chapter 16, describing Tom's behavior at the public dinner, Twain notes that nobody can be very ungraceful in nicely fitting beautiful clothes after he has grown a little used to them, especially if he is for the moment unconscious of them. This may be a comment on the self-conscious grandeur of an age in which fortunes were being made overnight by people who, like Tom, had been accustomed to very little.

In Chapter 12, describing the inhabitants of London Bridge, some of whom were born and died there without having set foot in any other part of the world, Twain might well have been writing about any provincials of his own time, who imagined that their small towns were the center of the universe.

SUBJECT BIBLIOGRAPHY AND GUIDE TO RESEARCH PAPERS

The Prince and the Pauper is found in numerous editions, many in paperback. Four paperback editions are brought out by the following publishers: Associated Booksellers ("Airmont"); Colliers Books; Dolphin Books; Harper and Row, Publishers, Inc.; New American Library of World Literature, Inc. ("Signet"); and Scholastic Book Services.

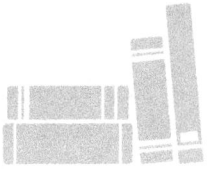

THE PRINCE AND THE PAUPER

CRITICAL BATTLE OVER MARK TWAIN'S PSYCHE

In the very early days, when Twain was still very much alive and writing, critics scorned his books, and libraries banned them for their vulgarity and "lack of consequence." Other of his contemporary critics praised him as the soul of American humor. In popular esteem, however, Mark Twain rode high, wide and handsome. He earned a fortune satisfying the tastes of the "great American populace" of the nineteenth and early twentieth centuries, while some segments of the intellectual leadership of the country looked on him with feelings of distaste that amounted almost to revulsion. In the main, Twain was revered "as America's funny man," and even after his death his work continued to command the respect of the majority of Americans.

EARLY OPINION

Some years after Twain's death in 1910, however, literary theorizing set in. Critics seemed to be less interested in what he wrote than in why he didn't write something else. Whether these theories resulted from a surfeit of Freud or from the wave of "anti-patriotism" that grew up in the twentieth century's disenchanted teens, or whether the theories arose from a mixture of these two and more, will probably never be known. At any rate, the major problem confronting students of Mark Twain's writings has come to be known as "Mark Twain's Wound."

BROOKS AND DE VOTO

In 1920 the critic Van Wyck Brooks published a volume entitled *The Ordeal of Mark Twain*. The work is based on Brooks' belief that the late-nineteenth and early-twentieth century cultural environment in America was not capable of sustaining artistic minds and helping them to grow and produce. Brooks' theory, simplified, is that the American cultural scene was too crassly materialistic to produce writers of great significance. He believed that important American literary men had to separate themselves from their native surroundings in order to allow their talents full room for development. Men like Henry James left America for other soils and climates more congenial to intellectual and artistic pursuits. Men like Ralph Waldo Emerson continued to live here, but separated themselves in spirit from strictly American ideals. They refused to restrict themselves to the intellectual attitudes narrowly characteristic of their native land.

In addition to these cultural drawbacks, Twain suffered from psychological experiences which left their mark on his sensitive personality. Further, Brooks felt that Mark Twain was a gifted writer, a man with a great talent, but a man who, unfortunately, had never allowed himself to develop his talent fully.

Searching Twain's biography, Brooks and his followers concluded that Mark Twain had chosen to gain popularity among the masses as "America's funny man," rather than to develop his skill as a serious writer. Twain's life long pursuit after riches and popularity was based on the not-necessarily-true American belief that wealth plus popularity equal success. That Twain chased riches is evident from the fact that he made much money which he invested in an unusual and striking house, and in business ventures (that often had little chance of success: an indication that Twain was no businessman, what he may have thought to the contrary notwithstanding). He rode to riches more than once in his lifetime. Each time he did so by becoming the "darling" of the popular audience. But by trying to appeal to the mass audience, Twain degraded wimself so that he was unable to write the "serious literature" he had it in him to write. The fault lies with the society which holds up the demon "wealth" as its badge of success.

Brooks and his followers saw other forces as contributing to the repression of Mark Twain's critical artistic skill. Among these were his wife's censorship and delicate literary prudery, and his friend's (William Dean Howells) insistence that he had a great comic talent. Not least of the stunting forces were Mark Twain's boyhood and young manhood days in Southern and Western backwaters among narrow, crude, and provincial people-including his own family, which unsuccessfully chased the rabbit of success like a pack of crippled hounds.

Writers who sided with Brooks in his comments were men like Waldo Frank, Malcolm Cowley, and Upton Sinclair.

DEFENSE OF TWAIN

Shortly after the appearance of Brooks' work, however, voices began to be heard in defense of Twain's artistry. These defenders held that far from being corrupted by his surroundings, Twain was helped by them. Mark Twain did not think America was crass and vulgar. Far from it; he considered American democracy and the spirit of free enterprise to be better systems than any the world had ever produced. It is obvious that he would not turn his barbed wit against the institutions he respected most. He did turn it against social institutions that he understood to be not honorable and not good. This is as much as we can expect from any man: that he be true to his ideals, whether they correspond to those of his society and age, or not.

Men like Carl Van Doren, Henry Seidel Canby, William Lyon Phelps, and Stephen Leacock took issue with Brooks' work. Their criticism ranged from Van Doren's remarks that Brooks had tried to psychoanalyze Twain and had failed, to Leacock's basic attitude that the West made Twain an artist, with the implication that without the West Twain would have been no artist.

Not until 1932, however, did anyone undertake a full scale frontal attack on Brooks' position. In that year, Bernard De Voto, in a book called *Mark Twain's America*, took the position that Twain was a writer of a specific kind of humor: the kind that was found in the works of Petroleum V. Nasby and Artemus Ward, the boisterous local humor of the American West. The loudness and brashness of Twain's work is due to the attitude of the Western frontiersman who not only loved the world and all that he saw in it, but also saw through to the realities of things with eyes uncluttered by the confusing forms that closed up the eyes of more pretentious Eastern writers.

The critical battle lines were drawn between critics who saw Twain as a successful-if superficial-humorist, and those who saw him as a tragic figure ironically hamstrung by the society whose adulation he craved and won.

RESOLUTION OF CRITICAL WAR

By 1975 the issue seemed to be settled in De Voto's favor. If Mark Twain was not a classical example of well adjusted humanity, neither was he a classic psychiatric basket case.

A valuable survey of the war between Brooks and De Voto is Lewis Leary's *Casebook on Mark Twain's Wound*, New York, 1962. Leary provides an introduction and survey of the problems, as well as generous selections from the writings of the critics who became involved.

Hudson Long also summarizes the dispute in his *Mark Twain Handbook*, New York, 1957, and in "Twain's Ordeal in Retrospect," *Southwestern Review* (1963), pp. 338-348.

Richard H. Powers agrees with Brooks in his "To Mark Twain's Missionary Defenders," *Forum* (1965), pp. 10-17. So does J. R. Vitelli in his "Introduction" to the 1970 reprint of Brooks' *The Ordeal of Mark Twain* (New York: E. P. Dutton).

CRITICAL REPUTATION OF "HUCKLEBERRY FINN"

The most important critical studies of Mark Twain's literary craftsmanship in the last thirty years have focused on *Huckleberry Finn*. The novel has come a long way from the days it was banned from the Concord (Mass.) Public Library for being "coarse," "inelegant," and "the veriest trash." Indeed, it draws more critical attention than any other work of Twain's.

HISTORY OF COMPOSITION

Walter Blair, for example, studied the chronological history of its composition, from the perspective of a critic interested in what was written and how it was done. His study (*Mark Twain and Huck Finn*, Berkeley: University of California Press, 1960) provides answers to many of the charges of literary bumbling and grossness brought against Twain in times past.

THE RIVER

No reader of *Huckleberry Finn* can be unaware of the tremendous flow of the Mississippi River. Some critics, notably T. S. Eliot and Lionel Trilling, have gone so far as to see in the River a kind of symbolic deity, a power sufficient to itself. The River "is not ethical or good," Trilling says, but it helps goodness grow in those people who make it an important element in their lives. It is from this general idea that Trilling develops the thesis that Huck is a servant of the River god.

Eliot maintains that the River dominates the structural form of the novel. The River is used metaphorically, structurally and thematically. Huck sees the big River gliding by and is suffused with a sense of awe and majestic calm. All the adventures begin and end on the River. Jim's freedom - the central point of the novel - involves a journey down the River. But at the same time the River does not determine Jim's freedom, Miss Watson does. And she represents the unthinking pietism and false values that Huck flees from not once, but twice: once when he leaves the Widow's house, and once again when he "lights out" for the Indian territory ahead of the rest because the Phelpses want to adopt him.

Both Eliot and Trilling use their conclusions to justify the ending of the novel which has been criticized as weak. Leo Marx points out that what truth there is in these critics' conclusions does not cover Twain's failure to face the philosophical point of his work. The novel ends weakly because Huck accepted Tom's game playing. Mark Twain, in other words, couldn't turn aside from his milieu. He had to free Jim even though Jim's freedom was meaningless in the context of Tom's shenanigans at the Phelps' plantation.

Lionel Trilling's essay, the "Introduction" to the Rinehart edition of *The Adventures of Huckleberry Finn* is reprinted in Trilling's *The Liberal Imagination*, New York, 1950. Trilling's views and those of T. S. Eliot (in his "Introduction" to the Chanticleer Press [Crown Publications] edition of *The Adventures of Huckleberry Finn*, New York, 1950) are discussed by Leo Marx in "Mr. Eliot, Mr. Trilling, and Huckleberry Finn," *American Scholar*, 21 (Autumn, 1953), 423-440.

A large proportion of academic effort and criticism has gone into studies that attempt to deal with the "problem" of the unsatisfactory ending. Most writers in the past 15 years feel that the ending is satisfactory; some feel it is an artistic achievement of the first order. (I can here only cite briefly some - and not always the best or most interesting-representative discussions that concern themselves one way or another with the ending. A quick check into one of the bibliographies listed at the end of the next section will provide the willing student with more material than he can handle.)

Among the better articles is one by Neil Schmitz ("Twain, Huckleberry Finn, and the Reconstruction," *American Studies*

[1971], pp. 59-67) which points out that after he is "freed" at the plantation Jim is in the circumstances and conditions of the freed slaves after the Civil War. The analysis Schmitz offers of Jim's condition indicates Mark Twain had a good grasp of his materials.

Chadwick Hansen ("The Character of Jim and the Ending of *Huckleberry Finn*," *Massachusetts Review*, [1963], pp. 45-66) says that Jim's character is the key to understanding the ending. He is raised from the lowest level of "comic stage Negro" to the highest type of character, the "Natural Man." In the end, when Huck and Jim decide to leave Arkansas, they are escaping from the lowest level of American culture to the last refuge of the "Natural," the Indian Territory. In such terms Hansen sees Jim's escape as a mythic act.

M. J. Sidnell ("Huck Finn and Jim: Their Abortive Freedom Ride," *The Cambridge Quarterly* [1967], pp. 203-211) argues on the one hand that neither Eliot nor Trilling faced up to the problem presented by Jim's treatment at Tom Sawyer's hands, and on the other hand that Marx was too ready to saddle Twain with a superficial sense of morality in opting for the ending. The final chapters, Sidnell points out, contain brutal ironies because Huck and Jim are more enslaved than ever.

Gerald Haslam (*Huckleberry Finn*: Why Read the Phelps Farm Episode?" *University of Washington Research Studies* [1967], pp. 189-197) indicates the last ten chapters are a fitting ending because they describe the moral dilemma of a slave state.

STRUCTURE

Treatments of technical aspects of composition and structure of *Huckleberry Finn* have focused on a number of topics. Among these is point of view. Two studies by Tony Tanner (Mark Twain and Wattie Bowser," *MTJ* [1963], pp. 1-6; and *The Reign of Wonder*, Cambridge: *Cambridge University Press*, 1965) and one by Horst H. Kruse ("Annie and Huck: A Note on *The Adventures of Huckleberry Finn*," AL [1967], pp. 207-214) indicate that Twain was aware of the advantages of using a child's point of view early in his career. He knew that such a viewpoint was effective for describing social injustice.

Alan Trachtenberg ("The Form of Freedom in Adventures of Huck Finn," *Southern Review* [1970], pp. 954-971) discusses Huck in his double role as a character in the story and as the teller of the story. Robert Regan's important book-length study (*Unpromising Heroes: Mark Twain and His Characters*, Berkeley: University of California Press, 1965) takes the approach of archetypal criticism in analyzing the characters of Twain's novels, among them Huck.

Analyses of the contrasts between social good and evil, innocence and experience, freedom and enslavement have provided material for many studies. William C. Spengemann (*Mark Twain and the Backwoods Angel*, Kent, Ohio: *Kent State University Press*, 1965) makes available much information concerning Twain's inability to accept or reject myths of America's innocence. Huck Finn is seen as an ideal innocent initiated into life; the contrast between the river and the shore serves to underscore Twain's attitude.

CHARACTER STUDIES

An unusual study is one by two psychiatrists, Jose Barchilar and Joel S. Kovel. "Huckleberry Finn: A Psychoanalytic Study (*Journal of the American Psychoanalytic Association* [1966], pp.

775-81e) appears to be a thorough, carefully done study which avoids the simplifications, easy generalizations and **cliches** usually found in such studies. The approach may not sit well with many literary scholars, but the article is suggestive.

Tom Sawyer comes in for study in Judith Fetterley's article "Disenchantment: Tom Sawyer in *Huckleberry Finn*," *PMLA* (1972), pp. 69-74. Fetterley contrasts the character of Tom in the two major Twain novels. She points out that the moral differences between the two Toms indicates a change in Twain's concept of the cruelty the boy perpetrates.

MATERIALISM

Neil L. Goldstein ("Mark Twain's Money Problems," Bucknell Review [1970], pp. 37-54) and Elizabeth McMahan ("The Money Motif: Economic Implications in *Huckleberry Finn*," *MTJ* [1971], pp. 5-10) discuss the use of money in Twain's work. Goldstein focuses on Twain's concern with money and material goods and its contrast with his ideals. McMahan indicates that Huck never lets money get in the way of his feelings in spite of their tightfistedness.

Articles that deal with other thematic concerns are Larry R. Dennis' "Mark Twain and the Dark Angel," in *Midwest Quarterly* [1967], pp. 181-197; and Neil Schmitz' "The Paradox of Liberation in *Huckleberry Finn*," *Texas Studies in Literature and Language* [1971], pp. 125-136. Schmitz deals with the meaning and application of freedom; Dennis with the fact of death. Dennis feels that Twain handles the problem best in HF because the character of Huck gave him direction.

SENTIMENTALISM

An interesting article that sheds light not only on the novel but also on Twain's philosophical perspective is James B. Lloyd's "The Nature of Mark Twain's Attack on Sentimentality in *The Adventures of Huckleberry Finn*" (*University of Mississippi Studies in English* [1972], pp. 59-63). Lloyd analyzes the kinds of crying done by the characters in the novel, pointing out that one group of criers is motivated by hate. Twain attacks the sentimental idea that human nature can be improved through appeals to the emotions.

Charles R. Metzger's "*The Adventures of Huckleberry Finn* as Picaresque" (*Midwest Quarterly* [1964], pp. 249-256) argues effectively that Huck has all the earmarks of a picaresque hero. This view should be balanced against that of Henry Nash Smith in his "Introduction" to the Riverside edition of the novel.

Lee A. Pederson's "Negro Speech in *The Adventures of Huckleberry Finn*" (*MTJ* [1965], pp. 1-4) analyzes Jim's speech and concludes that Mark Twain was a careful listener and an excellent recorder.

Finally, one item ought to be noted here as particularly useful. Alan Ostrom's "Huck Finn and the Modern Ethos" (*Centennial Review* [1972], pp. 162-179]) is a clearly written **exposition** of the novel as the account of Huck's inability to break free of the romantic and foolish attitudes and manners represented by Tom Sawyer. This is an excellent review of what is perhaps the most widely accepted view of the novel.

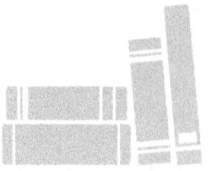

STUDY GUIDE

SUBJECT BIBLIOGRAPHY AND GUIDE TO RESEARCH PAPERS

The research paper should be based on careful reading of the texts of the original works which may be found in numerous editions, including paperback. Six paperback editions of *A Connecticut Yankee in King Arthur's Court* are brought out by the following publishers: Associated Booksellers ("Airmont"); Chandler Publishing Company; Harper and Row, Publishers, Inc.; Hill and Wang, Inc. ("American Century Series"); New American Library of World Literature, Inc. ("Signet"); and, Washington Square Press, Inc. Five paperback editions of *Life on the Mississippi* are available from the following publishers: Associated Booksellers ("Airmont"); Bantam Books, Inc.; Harper and Row, Publishers, Inc.; Hill and Wang ("American Century Series"); and, New American Library of World Literature, Inc. ("Signet"). Three paperbacks contain *The Mysterious Stranger*: *"The Mysterious Stranger" and Other Stories*, published by New American Library of World Literature, Inc. ("Signet"); *The Portable Mark Twain*, published by The Viking Press, Inc. ("Viking Paperbound Portables"); and, *The Complete Short Stories of Mark Twain*, published by Bantam Books, Inc.

There has been a great deal of criticism written about Mark Twain and his works. The following selective items include the most important criticism, with emphasis on *A Connecticut Yankee in King Arthur's Court*, *Life on the*

Mississippi, and *The Mysterious Stranger*. The bibliographical listings have been arranged alphabetically by author for each research topic:

GENERAL: STANDARD CRITICISM AND INTERPRETATION

Questions to consider: Has critical opinion altered since the original publication of these works? Consider the main targets of Twain's **satire**, such as his attacks on the established church and Sir Walter Scott. How is Twain's own personality revealed in these works? In what ways do these books differ from the writing of other authors of the same period?

Baldanza, Frank, *Mark Twain: An Introduction and Interpretation* (1961).

Boynton, Percy H., "Mark Twain," *Literature and American Life* (1936).

Brashear, Minnie M., *Mark Twain: Son of Missouri* (1934).

Brooks, Van Wyck, *The Ordeal of Mark Twain* (1920, 1933).

Calverton, V. F., *The Liberation of American Literature* (1932).

Canby, Henry Seidel, "Mark Twain," *Definitions* (Second Series) (1924).

Cardwell, Guy A., ed., *Discussions of Mark Twain* ("Discussions of Literature" series) (1963).

Chase, Richard, *The American Novel and Its Tradition* (1957).

Clark, Harry Hayden, "Mark Twain," *Eight American Authors: A Review of Research and Criticism*, ed., Floyd Stovall (1956, 1963).

____, ed., *Transitions in American Literary History* (1953).

Clemens, Samuel Langhorne, *Mark Twain's Speeches* (Introduction by Albert Bigelow Paine) (1910).

____, *The Complete Essays of Mark Twain*, ed., Charles Neider (1963).

____, *The Complete Humorous Sketches and Tales of Mark Twain*, ed., Charles Neider (1961).

____, *The Complete Short Stories of Mark Twain*, ed., Charles Neider (1957).

Compton, C. H., "Who Reads Mark Twain?" *Who Reads What?* (1934).

Cowie, A., "Mark Twain," *The Rise of the American Novel* (1948).

DeVoto, B. A., "Introduction," *Portable Mark Twain* (1946).

____, "Introduction to Mark Twain," *Literature in America*, ed., P. Rahv (1957).

____, *Mark Twain's America* (1932).

Ferguson, DeLancey, *Mark Twain: Man and Legend* (1943).

Fiedler, L. A., *Love and Death in the American Novel* (1960).

Foner, Philip S., *Mark Twain: Social Critic* (1958).

Gerould, G. H., "Explorers of Varying Scenes," *Patterns of English and American Fiction* (1942).

Hicks, Granville, "Mark Twain," *The Great Tradition* (1933).

Howard, Leon, *Literature and the American Tradition* (1960).

Johnson, Merle, *A Bibliography of the Works of Mark Twain, Samuel Langhorne Clemens* .... (1935).

Knight, Grant C., "Mark Twain," *American Literature and Culture* (1932).

_____, *The Critical Period in American Literature (1951).*

Leary, Lewis, *Articles on American Literature*, 1900-1950 (1954).

_____, *Mark Twain* (University of Minnesota, Pamphlets on American Writers) (1960).

Lewisohn, Ludwig, *Expression in America* (1932).

Long, E. Hudson, *Mark Twain Handbook* (1958).

Morley, C. D., "Hunting Mark's Remainders," *Streamlines* (1936).

Paine, A. B., *Mark Twain, A Biography* (3 volumes) (1912).

Parrington, Vernon Louis, "The Backwash of the Frontier - Mark Twain," *Main Currents in American Thought* (Volume 3) (1930).

Quinn, Arthur Hobson, *American Fiction: An Historical and Critical Survey* (1936).

Rubin, L. D., Jr., and J. R. Moore, eds., *The Idea of an American Novel* (1961).

Scott, Arthur L., *Mark Twain: Selected Criticism* (1955).

Smith, Henry Nash, *Mark Twain: A Collection of Critical Essays* (1963).

Snell, G. D., "Mark Twain," *Shapers of American Fiction*, 1798-1947 (1947).

Spiller, R. E., "Literary Rediscovery: Howells, Mark Twain," in *Cycle of American Literature*, ed., R. E. Spiller (1955).

Spiller, Robert E., and others, eds., *A Literary History of the United States* (1955).

Stovall, F., "Decline of Idealism," *American Idealism* (1943).

Taylor, W. F., *A History of American Letters* (1936).

_____, "Mark Twain," *The Economic Novel in America* (1942).

Van Doren, C. C. "Mark Twain," *The American Novel: 1789-1939* (1940).

Wagenknecht, E. C., "Lincoln of Our Literature," *Cavalcade of the American Novel* (1952).

_____, *Mark Twain: The Man and His Work* (1935).

Wecter, Dixon, *Sam Clemens of Hannibal* (1952).

A CONNECTICUT YANKEE IN KING ARTHUR'S COURT ANALYZED

Question to consider: In what ways does Twain make a satirical attack on the established church. Discuss Twain's attack on feudalism. Consider the points of view of the several storytellers who relate the story. Note the varieties of literary techniques used in this romance. Is there evidence that Twain is interested in "clothes philosophy"?

Baetzhold, H. G., "The Course of Composition of *A Connecticut Yankee*: A Reinterpretation," *American Literature* (1961).

Blair, Walter, *Horse Sense in American Humor* (1942).

Brooks, Van Wyck, *The Ordeal of Mark Twain* (1920, 1933).

Canby, H. S., *Turn West, Turn East* (1951).

Carter, Paul, "The Influence of W. D. Howells upon Mark Twain's Social Satire," *University of Colorado Studies* (1953).

Cox, J. M., "*A Connecticut Yankee in King Arthur's Court*: The Machinery of Self-Preservation," *Yale Review* (1960).

DeVoto, B., *Mark Twain's America* (1932).

Gibson, W. M., "Introduction" to *A Connecticut Yankee in King Arthur's Court* (1960).

Hill, Hamlin, "Introduction" to *A Connecticut Yankee in King Arthur's Court*.

Hoben, John, B., "Mark Twain's *A Connecticut Yankee*: A Genetic Study," *American Literature* (1946).

Lorch, Fred W., "Hawaiian Feudalism and Mark Twain's *A Connecticut Yankee in King Arthur's Court*" *American Literature* (1958R.

Moore, O. H., "Mark Twain and Don Quixote," *Publications of the Modern Language Association* (1922).

Neider, Charles, "Introduction" to *A Connecticut Yankee in King Arthur's Court* (1960).

Parrington, V. L., *Main Currents in American Thought* (1930).

Quinn, A. H., "Mark Twain and the Romance of Youth," *American Fiction* (1936).

Reiss, Edmund, "Afterword" to *A Connecticut Yankee in King Arthur's Court*.

Roades, Sister M. T., "*Don Quixote* and *A Connecticut Yankee*," *Mark Twain Quarterly* (1938).

Scott, A. L., "Mark Twain Looks at Europe," *South Atlantic Quarterly* (1953).

Sherman, Stuart P., "Mark Twain," *The Cambridge History of American Literature* (Volume 3), eds., W. P. Trent and others (1933).

Smith, Henry Nash, *Mark Twain's Fable of Progress: Political and Economic Ideas in A Connecticut Yankee* (1964).

Spiller, Robert E., and others, eds., *A Literary History of the United States* (1955).

Taylor, W. F., *The Economic Novel in America* (1942).

Wiggins, Robert A., "*A Connecticut Yankee* and *The Prince and The Pauper*: Structure and Meaning," *Mark Twain: Jackleg Novelist* (1964).

Wilson, R. H., "Malory in the Connecticut Yankee," *University of Texas Studies in English* (1948).

Winterich, John T., "Foreword" to *A Connecticut Yankee in King Arthur's Court* (1942).

LIFE ON THE MISSISSIPPI ANALYZED

Questions to consider: Contrast the two parts of the book as to the philosophic point of view of Mark Twain. Why does Twain introduce characters who actually lived? What is the role played by the Mississippi River in this work?

How does this work have an inspirational effect on the reader? How does Twain attack Sir Walter Scott?

Cairns, William B., *A History of American Literature* (1930).

Clemens, Samuel Langhorne, "Spring on the Mississippi," in *The American Year*, ed., H. H. Collins (1950).

DeVoto, B. A., "The River," *Mark Twain's America* (1951).

Ganzel, Dewey, "Twain, Travel Books, and Life on the Mississippi", *American Literature* (1962).

Gohdes, Clarence, "Mirth for the Million," *Literature of the American People* (1951).

Kriegel, Leonard, "Afterword" to *Life on the Mississippi* (1961).

Malone, D. H., "Analysis of Mark Twain's Novel Life on the Mississippi," in *The Frontier in American History and Literature*, ed., Hans Galinsky (1960).

Rankin, J. W., "Introduction" to *Life on the Mississippi* (1923).

Schmidt, Paul, "River vs. Town: Mark Twain's Old Times on the Mississippi," *Nineteenth - Century Fiction* (1960).

Scott, A. L., "Mark Twain Revises Old Times on the Mississippi," *Journal of English and Germanic Philology* (1955).

Sherman, Stuart P., "Mark Twain," *The Cambridge History of American Literature* (Volume 3), eds., W. P. Trent and others (1933).

Ticknor, C., "Mark Twain's Life on the Mississippi," *Glimpses of Authors* (1922).

Wagenknecht, Edward C., "Introduction" to S. L. Clemens' Life on the Mississippi (1944).

THE MYSTERIOUS STRANGER ANALYZED

Questions to consider: What is the evidence in this work that indicates Twain's pessimism? Does the reader feel sorry for young Satan? Are the **episodes** contrived? Does the ending of the story seem satisfying to the reader? Why was the tale set in the distant past? Is Twain's own youth reflected in this story?

Bellamy, Gladys C., *Mark Twain as a Literary Artist* (1950).

Cowper, F. A. G., "The Hermit Story, as Used by Voltaire and Mark Twain," in *Papers ... in Honor of ... Charles Frederick Johnson*, eds., Odell Shepard and Arthur Adams (1928).

DeVoto, B., "The Symbols of Despair," *Mark Twain at Work* (1942).

Ferguson, DeLancey, *Mark Twain: Man and Legend* (1943).

Fussell, E. S., "The Structural Problem of The Mysterious Stranger," *Studies in Philology* (1952).

Matthiessen, F. O., "Mark Twain at Work," *The Responsibilities of the Critic* (1952).

Parsons, C. O., "The Background of The Mysterious Stranger," *American Literature* (1960).

____, "The Devil and Samuel Clemens," *Virginia Quarterly Review* (1947).

Reiss, Edmund, "Afterword" to "The Mysterious Stranger" and Other Stories (1962).

Smith, H N., "Mark Twain's Images of Hannibal," University of Texas, Studies in English (1958).

ANALYSIS OF MARK TWAIN AS A PERSON

Questions to consider: Are Twain's Hannibal, Missouri and Mississippi River experiences reflected in his writings? How did his living in the West and his travels in Europe affect his point of view? How did Twain's years of residence in Connecticut influence his writings? Does Twain's viewpoint shift from optimism to pessimism?

Allen, Jerry, The Adventures of Mark Twain (1954).

Blankenship, Russell, "Mark Twain," American Literature (As an Expression of the National Mind) (1931).

Bolton, Sarah K., Famous American Authors (1954).

Bridges, H. J., "Pessimism of Mark Twain," As I Was Saying (1923).

Brooks, Van Wyck, "Mark Twain in the East," The Times of Melville and Whitman (1947).

____, "Note on Mark Twain," Chilmark Miscellany (1948).

____, The Confident Years: 1885-1915 (1952).

____, The Ordeal of Mark Twain (1920, 1933).

____, *The Times of Melville and Whitman* (1947).

Canby, H. S., "Homespun Philosophers," *Seven Years' Harvest* (1936).

Chesterton, G. K., "Mark Twain," in *Handful of Authors*, ed., G. K. Chesterton (1953).

Clemens, Samuel Langhorne, "Love Letters of Mark Twain," Jubilee (from *Atlantic Monthly*) (1957).

____, *Mark Twain's Notebook*, ed., Albert Bigelow Paine (1935).

____, *The Autobiography of Mark Twain*, ed., Charles Neider (1959).

Hagedorn, H., "Samuel Langhorne Clemens: 1835-1910," *Americans: A Book of Lives* (1946).

Herron, Ima Honaker, "Mark Twain and the Mississippi River Town," *The Small Town in American Literature* (1939).

Howells, W. D., "Boy of the Southwest," Jubilee (from *Atlantic Monthly*) (1957).

____, "Mark Twain," in *"Criticism and Fiction" and Other Essays*, eds., Clara Marburg Kirk and Rudolf Kirk (1959)

____, "My Mark Twain," in *Shock of Recognition*, ed., E. Wilson (1955).

Hubbell, J. B., "Mark Twain," *The South in American Literature*, 1607-1900 (1954).

Mencken, H. L., "H. L. Mencken on Mark Twain," in *Bathtub Hoax*, ed., H. L. Mencken (1958).

Morris, W., "Available Past: Mark Twain," in *Territory Ahead* (1958).

Priestley, J. B., "The Novelists," *Literature and Western Man* (1960).

Schmittkind, H. T. and D. A. Schmittkind, "Samuel Langhorne Clemens," *Living Biographies of Famous Novelist* (1943).

Untermeyer, L., "Mark Twain," in *Makers of the Modern World*, ed., L. Untermeyer (1955).

Van Doren, M., "Century of Mark Twain," *Private Reader* (1942).

Wagenknecht, E. C., ed., "Little Girl's Mark Twain," *When I Was a Child* (1946).

Wecter, Dixon, *Sam Clemens of Hannibal* (1952).

LITERARY TECHNIQUES USED BY MARK TWAIN

Questions to consider: What was Mark Twain's aim in writing this work? Which are the most effective of the literary techniques he uses? Consider Twain's choice of words and his ability to write good dialogue. Note the unexpected twists of thought in Twain's similes. Is humor introduced for a specific purpose? How is "contrast" used for literary purposes? How does Mark Twain weave recollections of his own past into his material?

Bellamy, Gladys Carmen, *Mark Twain As a Literary Artist* (1950).

Blair, Walter, *Native American Humor* (1937).

Branch, E. M., *The Literary Apprenticeship of Mark Twain* (1950).

Brashear, Minnie M., and Robert M. Rodney, eds., *The Art, Humor, and Humanity of Mark Twain* (1959).

Buxbaum, Katherine, "Mark Twain and American Dialect," *American Speech* (1927).

Canby, H. S., *Turn West, Turn East* (1951).

Clemens, Samuel Langhorne, "Fenimore Cooper's Further Literary Offenses," in *Heritage of American Literature* (Volume 2), eds., L. N. Richardson, G. H. Orians, and H. R. Brown (1951).

_____, "Fenimore Cooper's Literary Offenses," in *Shock of Recognition*, ed., E. Wilson (1955).

_____, *"How to Tell a Story" and Other Essays* (1897).

Cummings, Sherwood, "Science and Mark Twain's Theory of Fiction," *Philological Quarterly* (1958).

DeVoto, B. A., "Critics of Mark Twain," *Mark Twain's America* (1951).

_____, "Mark Twain and the Limits of Criticism," *Forays and Rebuttals* (1936).

_____, "Mark Twain: The Ink of History," *Forays and Rebuttals* (1936).

Fatout, Paul, *Mark Twain in Virginia City* (1964).

Feinstein, George, "Mark Twain's Idea of Story Structure," *American Literature* (1946).

Fraiberg, Louis, "Van Wyck Brooks versus Mark Twain versus Samuel Clemens," *Psychoanalysis and American Literary Criticism* (1960).

Fried, M. B., ed., *Mark Twain on the Art of Writing* (1961).

Gerber, J. C., "Relation Between Point of View and Style in the Works of Mark Twain," *Style in Prose Fiction*, ed., H. C. Martin (1959).

Goold, Edgar H., Jr., "Mark Twain on the Writing of Fiction," *American Literature* (1954).

Hoben, J. B., "Mark Twain: On the Writer's Use of Language," *American Scholar* (1956).

Hoffman, Daniel G., *Form and Fable in American Fiction* (1961).

Krause, S. L., "Twain's Method and Theory of Composition," *Modern Philology* (1959).

Lang, Andrew, "The Art of Mark Twain," in *Mark Twain: Selected Criticism*, ed., Arthur L. Scott (1955).

Lynn, Kenneth, *Mark Twain and Southwestern Humor* (1960).

Marx, L., "The Vernacular Tradition in American Literature," in *Studies in American Culture*, eds., J. J. Kwiat and M. C. Turpie (1960).

Matthews, Brander, "Mark Twain and the Art of Writing," *Essays on English* (1921).

Munson, Gorham B., "Prose for Humor and Satire," *Style and Form in American Prose* (1929).

Phelps, William Lyon, "The American Humorist: Mark Twain," *Some Makers of American Literature* (1923).

Rogers, F. R., *Mark Twain's Burlesque Patterns: As Seen in the Novels and Narratives, 1855-1885* (1960).

Rourke, Constance, *American Humor: A Study of the National Character* (1931).

Smith, H. N., *Mark Twain: The Development of a Writer* (1962).

Wagenknecht, E. C., *Mark Twain: The Man and His Work* (1935).

ANNOTATED BIBLIOGRAPHY

TEXTS AND EDITIONS

The standard scholarly editions of Mark Twain's writings are in the process of being edited. *The Mark Twain Papers*, a project of the University of California Press, is under the general editorship of Walter Blair, Donald Coney and Henry Nash Smith. This project calls for the publication of fourteen volumes of previously unpublished pieces by Twain, including items he himself rejected as well as business, personal, and literary correspondence. The first three volumes appeared in 1967, and others continue to appear.

John C. Gerber is chairman of the editorial board of the Iowa-California edition of the *Works of Mark Twain*. This series of twenty-five projected volumes is reprinting those works which have been published before.

A full description of these two projects was printed in "Twain in Progress: Two Projects" *American Quarterly* (1964), pp. 621-623.

The early collected edition of most of Twain's writings was edited in 1922-25 by Albert Bigelow Paine under the title *The Writings of Mark Twain*. These 37 volumes are in the collections of most libraries. The edition is flawed by uneven editing, and corrupt and tinkered texts.

The Family Mark Twain, published by Harper and Row, contains most of the major writings in one volume of over 1400 pages. Bernard DeVoto's *The*

Portable Mark Twain (New York: Viking Press, 1946, many times reprinted), though old, contains 785 pages of Twain plus an introductory essay by DeVoto.

PAPERBACKS

Paperback reprints of most of Twain's popular works are easy to come by, and many include introductions by critics and scholars. Dell has published a Laurel Edition (1960) of *The Adventures of Huckleberry Finn* with an introduction by Wallace Stegner. Houghton Mifflin's Riverside Edition (1958) has an introduction by Henry Nash Smith. W. W. Norton's annotated edition (reissued 1965) is helpful, as is the Scott, Foresman edition by James L. Bowen and Richard VanDerBeets (1970). Bowen and VanDerBeets print not only the text of the novel, but also a survey by E. M. Branch of the books written about it since the 1940s. They also print forty brief abstracts of critical articles. This is an extremely useful edition.

Hamlin Hill and Walter Blair's *The Art of Huckleberry Finn* (second ed. San Francisco: Chandler Publishing Co., 1969) is a reprint of the first American edition - the preferred copy-text - of the novel. The book also includes almost two hundred pages of introduction and scholarly criticism and comment.

Before making a commitment to use a paperback text of any of Twain's work, you should check two articles: Ruth Stein's "The A B C's of Counterfeit Classics: Adapted, Bowdlerized, Condensed," English Journal (1965), pp. 1160-1163; and John C. Gerber's "Practical Editions: Mark Twain's *The Adventures of Tom Sawyer* and *Adventures of Huckleberry Finn*," *Proof: Yearbook of American Bibliographical and Textual Studies* (1972), pp. 285-292. (Abstracted in 1972 *MLA Abstracts*, vol. I, item 8765.) Both Stein and Gerber note the unreliability of most classroom texts. Stein specifically reports on the use of word-lists and censorship in preparing the texts, while Gerber indicates the texts' general unreliability: there is no text of Tom Sawyer without corruptions, and texts of *Huckleberry Finn* based on the Author's National or Limp Leather editions contain as many as 2600 variants.

BIOGRAPHIES-GENERAL

Biographies of Mark Twain range from Paine's *Mark Twain: A Biography* (3 vols., New York, 1912), which has the advantages of being an "official" biography and of having been published within two years of Twain's death; to Justin Kaplan's *Mr. Clemens and Mark Twain* (New York: Simon and Schuster, 1965) which has the advantage of having won a Pulitzer Prize. Kaplan's book has practically become the standard biography and supports the general impression of the split between Clemens and Twain.

Jerry Allen's *The Adventures of Mark Twain* (New York, 1954) offers a readable narrative but, like Douglas Grant's *Mark Twain* (New York: Grove Press, 1962), is less specialized in style and approach than Kaplan's work.

DeLancey Ferguson's *Mark Twain: Man and Legend* (New York, 1943; reissued Indianapolis, Bobbs-Merrill, 1963) has long been one of the best around.

BIOGRAPHIES - JUVENILE

For young readers Monroe Stearns' *Mark Twain* (New York: Franklin Watts, 1965) and Earl S. Miers' *Mark Twain on the Mississippi* (New York: Collier, 1963) are acceptable, though Miers' is fictionalized.

A suggested corrective to Miers is Lucian R. Smith's article "Sam Clemens: Pilot," (MTJ [1971], pp. 1-5), which suggests some reasons why Twain didn't go back to steamboats after the Civil War.

BIOGRAPHIES - LIMITED SCOPE

Some other works give valuable information about specific periods or specific aspects of Twain's life. Dixon Wecter (*Sam Clemens of Hannibal*, Boston,

1952) provides much information about Twain's childhood in Hannibal. Paul Fatout's *Mark Twain in Virginia City* (Bloomington: Indiana University Press, 1964) does an excellent job of covering the period between September, 1862 and May 1864.

A picture of the Clemens family between 1872 and 1896 is provided in Edith Colgate Salisbury's *Family Dialogues: Susy and Mark Twain* (New York: Harper and Row, 1965). Salisbury uses selections from Twain family writings to provide the dialogue that illustrates their relationships.

Leah Strong recounts the influence of the Rev. Joe Twichell in *Joseph Hopkins Twichell, Mark Twain's Friend and Pastor* (Athens, Ga.: University of Georgia Press, 1965). Twain's relationship with his publisher is documented in Hamlin Hill's *Mark Twain and Elisha Bliss* (Columbia, Mo.: University of Missouri Press, 1964).

Fred W. Lorch, *The Trouble Begins at Eight: Mark Twain's Lecture Tours* (Ames, Iowa: Iowa State University Press, 1968) and Paul Fatout, *Mark Twain on the Lecture Circuit* (Bloomington: Indiana University Press, 1960) are mutually complementary studies of Twain's public speaking career.

PERSONAL ATTITUDES

Margaret Duckett's *Mark Twain and Bret Harte* (Norman, Oklahoma: University of Oklahoma Press, 1964) indicates that Twain was probably the cause of the trouble between the two writers. Her conclusions are supported by Hamlin Hill's "Mark Twain and His Enemies," (*Southern Review* [1968], pp. 520-529) which notes the importance of fear as a motivating force in Twain's complex personality.

Harold Baetzhold traces Twain's shifting attitude toward England and Englishmen in *Mark Twain and John Bull: the British Connection* (Bloomington: University of Indiana Press, 1970).

Paul Baender suggests that a crucial event in the development of Twain's outlook on life may be a fiction in "Alias Macfarlane: A Revision of Mark Twain Biography" (AL [1965], pp. 187-197).

PERSONAL RECOLLECTIONS

Marylin Austin Baldwin edited William Dean Howells' affectionate *My Mark Twain: Reminiscences and Criticisms* (Baton Rouge: Lousiana State University Press, 1967). She includes other essays by Howells pertaining to Twain. Justin Kaplan's abridged version of Howells' work, called *Mark Twain: a Profile* (New York: Hill and Wang, 1967), contains essays by other writers. Other personal reminiscences of Mark Twain are provided by Clara Clemens' *My Father, Mark Twain* (New York, 1931).

Finally, but very important, are Henry Nash Smith's *Mark Twain: The Development of a Writer* (Cambridge, Mass.: Harvard University Press, 1962) and Edward Wagenknecht's *Mark Twain: The Man and His Work* (3rd ed. Norman, Oklahoma: University of Oklahoma Press, 1967). Smith discusses Twain as a craftsman and thinker, and illustrates the two sides frequently noted in Twain's personality. Wagenknecht's third edition includes a "Commentary on Mark Twain Criticism and Scholarship since 1960" as well as a bibliography. The book is valuable as a starting point for study of Mark Twain.

The Brooks-DeVoto debate has been summarized in a separate section above, but it should be noted that DeVoto's *Mark Twain's America* (Boston: Little, Brown, 1932) contains a great deal of important background information, as does Brooks' *The Ordeal of Mark Twain* (New York, 1920, rev., 1933, rev. ed. reissued 1970).

HUMOR

Constance Rourke provides background for an understanding of Mark Twain's place in the annals of American humor in *American Humor: A Study of the National Character* (New York, 1931). Two recent studies also focus on Twain's humor. Pascal Covici, Jr., examines the ways Twain used humor to draw the reader's attention to the human predicament in his *Mark Twain's Humor* (Dallas: Southern Methodist University Press, 1962). James M. Cox, *Mark Twain and the Fate of Humor* (Princeton: Princeton University Press, 1965) suggests that Mark Twain was at his best when working according to the "pleasurable principle." Cox's book is quite good.

LITERARY ARTISTRY

Studies of Mark Twain as a literary artist are getting more plentiful. Gladys Bellamy's *Mark Twain as a Literary Artist* (Norman, Oklahoma: University of Oklahoma Press, 1950) set the stage for studies of Twain as an artist. Lewis Leary's *Mark Twain* (Minneapolis: University of Minnesota Press, 1960) and Edgar M. Branch's *The Literary Apprenticeship of Mark Twain* (Urbana: University of Illinois Press, 1950) also deal with the literary artistry of Twain and its development.

An abridged version of Maxwell Geismar's *Mark Twain, An American Prophet* is available from McGraw-Hill (1969) in paperback. The study provides a chronological analysis of Twain's work "in its biographical context" and a critique of Twain as a "literary master and a cultural hero."

In *Mark Twain, Jackleg Novelist* (Seattle: University of Washington Press, 1964), Robert A. Wiggins suggests that Twain was an improviser who did his best work when writing realistic and humorous work. Hamlin Hill shows how

Twain's techniques fit a certain kind of publishing operation, the subscription house, which required sensational material ("Mark Twain: Audience and Artistry," *American Quarterly* [1963], pp. 25-40].

LITERARY CRITICISM

A recent full length study of Twain's literary criticism is Sydney J. Krause's *Mark Twain as Critic* (Baltimore: Johns Hopkins Press, 1967).

SOCIAL PHILOSOPHY

As a social commentator, Twain has drawn the attention of many writers. Three important studies are: Louis J. Budd's *Mark Twain, Social Philosopher* (Bloomington; University of Indiana Press, 1962), a broad but complete study of the novelist's social thought; Thomas Blues' *Mark Twain and the Community* (Lexington: University of Kentucky Press, 1970), an analysis of Twain's understanding of the relationship between the individual and his society; and Mary E Goad's *The Image and the Woman in the Life and Writings of Mark Twain* (Emporia State Research Studies [1974], pp. 5-70).

COLLECTIONS OF CRITICAL ESSAYS

Several collections make critical essays available outside library walls. The earliest is Arthur Scott's *Mark Twain: Selected Criticism* (Dallas, 1955). Guy Cardwell's *Discussions of Mark Twain* is in the *D. C. Heath* "Discussions of Literature" series (1963). Prentice-Hall is represented by Henry Nash Smith's *Mark Twain: A Collection of Critical Essays* (1963) in its "Twentieth Century Views" series, and by Claude Simpson's *Twentieth Century Interpretations of Adventures of Huckleberry Finn* (1968). All these include useful introductions and carefully chosen discussions.

Frederick Anderson's *Mark Twain, The Critical Heritage* (New York: Barnes and Noble, 1971) reprints 88 reviews and evaluations of Twain from 1869-1913. British and American materials are included.

Lewis Leary's essays are reprinted in his *Southern Excursions, Essays on Mark Twain and Others* (Baton Rouge: Louisiana State University Press, 1971). David B. Kesterson edited *Critics on Mark Twain* (Coral Gables: University of Miami Press, 1973). Dean Morgan Schmitter's *Mark Twain* is a McGraw-Hill paperback in that company's "Contemporary Studies in Literature" series (1974).

BIBLIOGRAPHIES

In addition to the bibliographies and bibliographical notes in the works already mentioned, lists of works about Twain are found in the following:

Abstracts of English Studies. Boulder, Colorado: National Council of Teachers of English. Appears monthly.

American Literary Scholarship. An Annual, 1963-. Durham, N. C.: Duke University Press. Chapter 5 contains a selective critical bibliography of Twain studies.

Asselineau, Roger, *The Literary Reputation of Mark Twain from 1910 to 1950*. New York, 1956.

Beebe, Maurice and John Feaster. "Criticism of Mark Twain: A Selected Check List." This appeared in the special *Huckleberry Finn* issue of *Modern Fiction Studies* (Spring, 1968), pp. 93-139.

Clark, Harry Hayden and Howard Baetzhold, "Mark Twain" in *James Woodress*, ed. *Eight American Authors: A Review of Research and Criticism*. Revised. New York: W. W. Norton, 1971.

Leary, Lewis. *Articles on American Literature*, 1900-1950. Durham, N. C.: Duke University Press, 1954.

_____, et al. *Articles on American Literature*, 1950-1967. Durham, N. C.: Duke University Press, 1970.

MLA Abstracts. New York: Modern Language Association. An annual, publishes abstracts prepared by the authors of the items.

MLA International Bibliography. Vol. I. New York: Modern Language Association. Look under "American Literature IV. Nineteenth Century, 1870-1900. Clemens."

Schmitter, Dean Morgan. "Annotated Bibliography," *Mark Twain, A Collection of Criticism*. New York: McGraw-Hill, 1974.

Spiller, Robert, et al. *Literary History of the United States*. 4th ed. New York; Macmillan, 1974.

www.ingramcontent.com/pod-product-compliance
Lightning Source LLC
LaVergne TN
LVHW011729060526
838200LV00051B/3096